The Force Is in the Mind

Elke Krasny
Architekturzentrum Wien

The Force
Is in the Mind
The Making of
Architecture

Az W

BIRKHÄUSER
BASEL · BOSTON · BERLIN

Published by Elke Krasny, Architekturzentrum Wien

Director: Dietmar Steiner
Business manager: Karin Lux

**This book was published to accompany the exhibition
"Architektur beginnt im Kopf. The Making of Architecture"
Oct. 16, 2008 to Feb. 02, 2009 at the Architekturzentrum Wien.**

Curator of the exhibition: Elke Krasny
Project coordination and research assistance: Gudrun Hausegger
Research assistance: Robert Temel
Scenography: Alexandra Maringer
Assistant: Bernadette Krejs
Setting: Dietlind Rott
Graphic design: Thomas Kussin, buero8

Editor: Elke Krasny (ek)
Authors: Gudrun Hausegger, Elke Krasny, Robert Temel (rt), Dietmar Steiner, Gerhard Vana
Two object descriptions: Peter G. Auer, Manfred Wolff-Plottegg
Translation: James Roderick O'Donovan

Graphic design of the book and typesetting: o- Alexander Schuh
Digital imaging: Martina Frühwirth, o- Alexander Schuh
Copyediting: Andrea M. Werther

Front cover: Orchid, Lacaton & Vassal, Paris © Elke Krasny
Proportional compass, Archive Vana-Architekten, Vienna, © Peter Kubelka
Back cover: Wooden triangle, Lux Guyer, Zurich © Peter Kubelka
Colour pencils, Diller Scofidio + Renfro, New York © Peter Kubelka
Credits and sources: see details in the captions. We have taken great pains to ensure that all
credits are accurate and complete. However, should any photographer feel that their rights
have been infringed by the omissions of their name, please contact the Architekturzentrum Wien.

Neither the catalogue nor the exhibition would have been possible without the generous support
of public and private collections and archives in lending us material.

    bm:uk ARCHITECTURE LOUNGE Architekturzentrum Wien   Institut Français de Vienne

Bibliographic information published by the German National Library
The German National Library lists this publication in the Deutsche Nationalbibliografie; detailed
bibliographic data are available on the Internet at http://dnb.d-nb.de.

This book has also been published in a German language edition (ISBN 978-3-7643-8979-6).

© 2008
Architekturzentrum Wien and authors
Birkhäuser Verlag AG
Basel · Boston · Berlin
P.O. Box 133, CH-4010 Basel, Switzerland
Part of Springer Science+Business Media

Printed on acid-free paper produced from chlorine-free pulp. TCF ∞
Printed by: Holzhausen Druck & Medien GmbH, Vienna

Printed in Austria

ISBN 978-3-7643-8980-2

9 8 7 6 5 4 3 2 1

Content

How does architecture arise? Initially, in the mind, or so we contend. Then the idea is formulated using tools. We say tools because as a kind of extension of thoughts and ideas, they both codify and communicate these. And because the tools employed help to determine the end result. For instance, in the 1960s it was usual to sketch with a thick pencil, the famous 6B lead. At that time plans were produced in the form of glossy prints and were covered with coloured films. In the 1990s the first architecture gallery in London called itself, in contrast, 9H, the thinnest and hardest pencil lead. There can be no doubt that the tools used to formulate ideas permit us to draw conclusions about the built architecture. When years earlier in the 1970s I rejected the rounded corners, the thick felt pens and the glossy prints and started to draw again with coloured pencils on tracing paper this was also a rejection (that I regarded as revolutionary) of earlier architecture. The relationship between head, hand and tool was very clear at that time. Back then I discussed with Bruno Reichlin late into the night the question about what position is adapted if one draws a line and then has to decide how to continue it around the corner. Considerations of this kind were over when the first drawing computers conquered architects' offices, as initially they could only draw straight lines. And now we compare the architecture of this period with the flowing forms of today and can answer the question by saying that it is also the design tools that determine the idea and forms of architecture.

For, all the tools and the techniques used to present and convey an idea have their technical possibilities, limitations and conditions. Consequently, is architecture perhaps not just what is thought up in the mind or dreamt of, but also those things that can be visually conveyed with the tools available at the particular time? Elke Krasny's approach of selecting architecture offices for this project on the basis of their different ways of working both opens up and deciphers this problem. A unique glimpse, through a keyhole, of the intimacy of the production of architecture. One could easily believe one is attending an act of creation…

Dietmar Steiner

GARY COOPER ALS ARCHITEKT HOWARD ROARK IM FILM „THE FOUNTAINHEAD" (EIN MANN WIE SPRENGSTOFF) 1949, PHOTO: CINETEXT

HERMANN CZECH

ATELIER BOW-WOW

LACATON & VASSAL

YONA FRIEDMAN

PHOTOS: ELKE KRASNY

VILÉM FLUSSER

„However, tools do not change only the environment but also humankind, their users. They impact on their users who simulate their own simulators."

Of Tools and Inspiration.
The Economies of Architectural Creativity

Elke Krasny

a) Orchid, b) a rifle, c) pieces of Lego, d) cigarette ash, e) a bed, f) rustic chests, g) trees, h) watercolours, i) solutions from the history of architecture, j) words, k) taking a stroll, l) cinema, m) suspended cords, … what may appear like the shattering of "all plans" that occurs in Michel Foucault's The Order of Things in which he introduces a) a "certain Chinese encyclopaedia (…), (…) b) embalmed animals, c) tamed ones, d) pigs, e) sirens, e) mythical beasts," (FOUCAULT 1971: 17) is, in fact, an initial approach to the instruments encountered in architects' offices that are used in the act of designing to discover ideas. What counts is the moment, on occasions almost mythically transfigured, when the act of designing starts. In the conversations with men and women architects it was revealed that the question about the procedure of design, or about when the design reaches its end, is one that is rarely posed.

In 2006 when I embarked upon my architectural field research for The Force Is in the Mind. The Making of Architecture, I had the following question in my mind: how do the relationships and constellations between architects, their tools and their work spaces combine in the process of designing?

I had a suspicion that the way in which tools are used exerts an influence upon the design act, its course, the way it is represented and, ultimately, on the architecture itself. I saw the architects' offices or studios as multi-dimensional visiting cards, not in the sense of a representative gesture but more in the sense of deep, fundamental approaches and philosophies that emerge on the surface in spatial terms.

Questions about "how" were used as a basis for "what". The issue was not so much what architects do but how they do it. At the same time I was interested in the different combinations of the tools used and their influences, as, in terms of how things are done, these play a decisive role for possible ways of thinking, both as regards delight in overstepping boundaries and criticism of the boundaries themselves. What roles do collective tools play in an era of the individual design act? How have computer programmes, for example, changed design methods?

"Since the turn of the century, scores of men and women have penetrated deep forests, lived in hostile climates, and weathered hostility, boredom, and disease in order to gather the remnants of so called primitive societies. By contrast to the frequency of these anthropological excursions, relatively few attempts have been made to penetrate the intimacy of life among tribes that are much nearer at hand." (LATOUR, WOOLGAR 1986: 17) This is how Bruno Latour and Steve Woolgar describe their venture into the laboratory. Laboratory Life became atelier life

EDGE DESIGN INSTITUTE · EDGE DESIGN INSTITUTE · R&SIE(N) · R&SIE(N)

PHOTOS: EDGE DESIGN INSTITUTE, R&SIE(N)

GILLES DELEUZE, CLAIRE PARNET

"Tools always presuppose a machine and this is always a primarily social machine. A tool remains peripheral or hardly used as long as no social machine or collective concatenation exists."

RUDOLF OLGIATI'S COLLECTION OF ANTHROPOLOGICAL OBJECTS,
OLGIATI STIFTUNG, FLIMS

for the project 'The Force Is in the Mind', in the form of contemporary instant field work. Visits to offices extending over a period of several days, watching architects at work, documentary photographs, taking part in discussions with clients, in design sessions, staff organisational meetings, as well as conversations and interviews were the tools I chose for my studio field research. In the case of architects no longer alive interviews with former members of their staff provided an approach to these architects' way of working.

Research in Alvar Aalto's studio revealed that no researcher had ever enquired about what tools Aalto used. Even a collection of hundreds of sketches on a project offers no information about the course taken by the design process, if it is not possible to talk to still living members of the office staff. This failure to be aware of the necessity of talking about the making of architecture as a key to deciphering the courses taken by design and the development of ideas, matches the puzzling relationship between paper and what is drawn upon it described by Mark Wigley: "We have been trained to act as if the paper is not present, trained to see through it, noticing only the dark marks made upon it." (WIGLEY 2005: 331) The relationship between lines and paper first became visible through the fact that, in the 1960s, architecture drawn on paper, following the new model of the black screen with white lines, was republished in white on black. Whereas this is a technological act that allows us perceive a relationship and something that is simply absent as it is taken for granted, in my ears it is speaking, the 'oral history' of architecture, that allows the absent element in the process, the work, to have its say.

To connect speaking and looking visits were made to the following studios: Alvar Aalto in Jyväskylä and Helsinki, Lina Bo Bardi in São Paulo, Bow-Wow in Tokyo, Hermann Czech in Vienna, Diller Scofidio + Renfro in New York, Edge Design Institute in Hong Kong, Yona Friedman in Paris, Antoni Gaudí in Barcelona, Lux Guyer in Zurich, Steven Holl Architects in New York, The Jerde Partnership in Los Angeles, Lacaton & Vassal in Paris, Rudolf Olgiati in Flims, Charlotte Perriand in Paris, R&Sie(n) in Paris, Schwalm-Theiss in Vienna, Karl Schwanzer in Vienna, Skidmore, Owings & Merrill SOM in Chicago, UNStudio in Amsterdam and Venturi Scott Brown & Associates VSBA in Philadelphia.

The counterpart in this dialogue was provided by research into the typical tools of the architecture profession in the 20th century, as found in private collections, firms as well as in museums, none of which, clearly, has specialised in this particular area of collecting. The collective production of knowledge represented by architecture as stored in the tools, and the

YONA FRIEDMAN   THE JERDE PARTNERSHIP   UNSTUDIO   ATELIER BOW-WOW

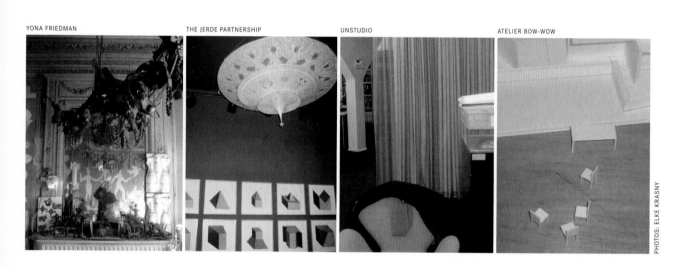

PHOTOS: ELKE KRASNY

SANFORD KWINTER

"Our task, I would argue, is to resist these pathways of thought, and wherever possible to expand the concept of the concrete and to extend the play of intuition into new domains."

ALVAR AALTO, SKETCH UNIVERSITY OF TECHNOLOGY, OTANIEMI 1949–1974
ARCHIVES OF THE ALVAR AALTO MUSEUM, JYVÄSKYLÄ

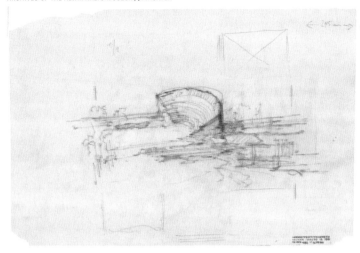

attempt made through field research to give this knowledge a voice in the respective design methods reveals that making architecture is a practice full of contradictions between standards and departures from them, internalised norms and deliberate infringements.

"Through architects the art of architecture has sunk to the level of a graphic art. It is not those who can build best that receive the most commissions but those whose work looks best on paper. (...) And therefore the adept presenter rules. It is no longer the work tool held in the hand that creates forms, but the pencil. From the outlines of a building, from the kind of ornament, the observer can tell whether the architect worked with pencil number 1 or with pencil number 5." This observation by Adolf Loos sounds contemporary, effortlessly makes the leap across a time distance of 100 years, and accurately describes the render generation. (© UTE WOLTRON). This strengthens the suspicion that it is an undertone of cultural pessimism that formulates this criticism of the tool as the decisive moment of change, because this moment avoids being controlled. It is precisely this loss of control that arouses the suspicion that something is not produced by mastery or ability but by the arbitrary quality of the tool.

Although today we still tend to ascribe to the computer the power of the visualisation that promises everything and the form finding that can do everything, the euphoria of the 1990s, when the computer seemed to be the tool of the future, already held in the hand, has by now given way to a more hybrid range of instruments.

If speed is the force that, in the form of the omnipresent time factor, propels all design processes in the world, it is precisely in the context of this scrimmage that reaching for a pencil, the quickly recorded variation made with a marker on the tracing paper, or the small sketch book taken out while on the move have once more become privileged.

Essentially, we can discern two major directions. Whereas one is based always on the immaterial, on speaking, reflecting, considering before making the first line, in the other architecture is worked out precisely through these lines, through sketching, directed by the imagination, hand and eye and inscribed on a medium. The potential offered by computer programmes reduces the creative gap but at the same time increases the pressure of individualisation and innovation on each person.

In reflecting on the fact that one cannot rely on a single tool alone but that, in fact, one allows the interplay of many tools, intuitively, spontaneously, in an improvised controlled, focussed, or unconscious way lies the daily experience of work that repeatedly endeavours to provide its own methods and must affirm its own approach.

VENTURI SCOTT BROWN & ASSOCIATES

EDGE DESIGN INSTITUTE

STEVEN HOLL ARCHITECTS

DILLER SCOFIDIO + RENFRO

PHOTOS: ELKE KRASNY, GUDRUN HAUSEGGER

"The 'invention' of the tools makes manifest the 'finding' of the ideas."

LEFT: GAUDÍS STUDIO HUT, SAGRADA FAMÍLIA. RIGHT: RECONSTRUCTION

As regards the questions about starting to design, about the sources of inspiration, the individual steps in the work process and, not least importantly, about the evaluation of the role of the computer, the answers given by the various positions selected for this book open up architectural histories of a different kind that indicate the omissions made by standard architectural history in the form of canonical histories of form and style without any technological or cultural perspective. Consequently, one could divide the history of architecture into very different epochs, starting from a scientific historical logic of the technology of the tools and architects' attitude to them. From this attitude there results action that in the act of designing produces something that permissively transcends the tool and places the emphasis on the power of thought. This, precisely, is where the starting point (always newly defined) lies for a tentative approach to a "personal handwriting". It is found again in the attempt to fully realize the individual relationship to the participating, already existing or "invented" design actants: a) orchids, b) a rifle, c) pieces of Lego, d) cigarette ash, e) a bed ...

REFERENCES

Foucault, Michel (1971) Die Ordnung der Dinge. Eine Archäologie der Humanwissenschaften, Frankfurt am Main: Suhrkamp.

Latour, Bruno and Steve Woolgar (1986) Laboratory Life. The Construction of Scientific Facts, Princeton: Princeton University Press.

Wigley, Mark (2005) Back to Black, in Brayer, Marie-Ange, Frederick Migayrou and Fumio Nanjo (Ed.) ArchiLab's Urban Experiments. Radical Architecture, Art and the City, Ed., London Thames & Hudson.

Loos, Adolf (1910) Wiener Architekturfragen 1910, in Opel, Adolf (Hg.) (1995) Adolf Loos, Über Architektur. Ausgewählte Schriften und Originaltexte, Wien: Georg Prachner Verlag.

de Certeau, Michel (1988) Kunst des Handelns, Berlin: Merve.

Gänshirt, Christian (2007) Werkzeuge für Ideen. Einführung ins architektonische Entwerfen, Basel, Boston and Berlin: Birkhäuser.

Piedmont-Palladino, Susan C. (2007) Tools of the Imagination: Drawing Tools and Technologies from the Eighteenth Century to the Present, New York: Princeton Architectural Press.

ARCHITECTURAL FIELDWORK: TWENTY STUDIO VISITS

The Creator created paper to draw architecture on

Alvar Aalto 1898–1976

1955–1976 Atelier Tiilimäki 20
Helsinki
Finland

Research in the Alvar Aalto Archive in Jyväskylä as well as in
Aalto's home and the Aalto studio in Helsinki in June 2008,
photography, discussions with Vezio Nava, Georg Schwalm-Theiss,
Marjo Holma and Marja-Liisa Hänninen & text: Elke Krasny

"The secretary gave him six or seven 6Bs. The maestro put them in his vest. This was like having a pistol, now he was armed. He came up, stopped at different tables, then he would take one pencil, did some corrections and always left the pencil on the table, and then took the next one and forgot it again. And the secretary would come later to collect all the pencils for the next round," Vezio Nava, who worked in Alvar Aalto's studio from 1961 to 1984 describes a typical morning there. The famous 6B was a yellow clutch pencil made by Koh-i-Noor. In the Aalto Archive in Jyväskylä one such pencil and two boxes containing leads for it are preserved like precious objects. In Aalto's former studio in Helsinki, at no. 20 Tiilmäki, if you open the drawers of a low piece of wooden office furniture on the ground floor, opposite the stairs leading to the drawing studio, you are surprised by a wealth of tools. Until his death in 1976 Aalto headed this studio, which was then directed by his second wife, Elissa Aalto, until 1994. In the office, today used as its base by the Alvar Aalto Foundation and practically unchanged, it is not individual items with a particular aura that have been preserved but the everyday supply of tools for an architect's office that has been frozen at a specific point in time, so to speak. Many of the items are still in their original packaging. In addition to a number of letter stamps used for lettering drawings, many different kinds of compasses, mechanical pencils, leads in different degrees of hardness, Rotring drawing ink and Rapidographs, Pelikan Graphos pens, sandpaper stretched on a piece of wood, hard round erasers, plastic French curves, templates and razor blades there are also two little boxes containing yellow 6B clutch pencils and package upon package of the leads used in these pencils.

The studio in Munkkiniemi on the periphery of Helsinki, near Laajalahti Bay, was designed by Aalto between 1954 and 1955 and even during his lifetime was visited by "architecture aficionados" from throughout the world, including India and Japan. The situation today is not much different: from Monday to Friday, at precisely 12.30 p.m. the studio door is opened to international architecture tourists. A bare 500 metres away Aino (his first wife who died in 1949) and Alvar Aalto had their home and studio from 1936 onwards. When one visits it today it seems to have survived practically in its original condition. The drawing tables are covered with materials, sketches and plans and T-squares as well as large rulers hang on the walls. In the 1950s Aalto had an office in Ratakatu in central Helsinki, in the "Engineers Building" that he designed himself, as well as a further one in Rovaniemi, in northern Finland. The number of staff had grown to 24. Among Aalto's arguments for building a new studio was that he wanted to offer international architects somewhere to work and to build up an

ELISSA AALTO ON ALVAR AALTO'S WORKING PRACTICE

"When you look at the earlier drawings, it looks as if he is using drawings to find solutions and forms. When he was older, I think he did more mental work."

academy of architecture en miniature. The courtyard with stone steps that resembles an amphitheatre and a white wall for showing slide projections and films in front of Aalto's personal office (known by the staff as his "Ateljee") were intended for the academy that only partially came to fruition. The magisterial bird's eye view from the balcony-like platform in Aalto's office allowed the huge drawings or models placed on the desk to be analysed. Clients were also received at this desk, which, along with the chairs, came from the Artek company founded by Aino and Alvar Aalto in 1935. In the 1960s the mayor of Helsinki was a frequent visitor here. "You have to know the personality of Alvar Aalto. He had a great charisma, a great ego, he was a showman, an actor, he liked to play, to show off." If clients had doubts, Aalto always had an absolutely impossible solution in reserve so as to convince them of the solution that he secretly favoured. "He was a good conductor, a good director. He pumped confidence into his collaborators saying: When I am not here, you are like Alvar Aalto," recalls Nava, describing the way in which this maestro directed his employees, all of whom sat in the open-plan office. On the space divider walls behind every desk there were wooden tracks to hang plans and drawings on. Initially, in addition to the two architects office lamps above every desk, the only other source of light was subtly directed daylight, in summer curtains provided protection against excessive sunlight. More lamps were fitted in response to the requests of the staff. Books on architecture or specialist magazines were not used as reference sources, Aalto had his library at home, in the office there was only information on technical or legal matters. The gleaming white of the walls, the brown of the drawing tables and plan chests, the black upholstery of the chairs create an atmosphere that radiates a plain, pleasant sense of order.

"The office was not so strict. There was not such a strict hierarchy. Aalto was proud that only architects and architectural students worked in his office, no draughtsmen. Normally there was a chief architect leading a crew of five architects. Sometimes there were even

smaller groups. And there were ten model boys. There were always two Swiss architects in the office." The atmosphere at work was pleasant, the rhythm of work alternated between intensive phases and "demi force," as Aalto like to call it. In summer people sat outside on the stone steps. When Aalto invited staff to talk to him in the "taverna" that was added in 1963 they drank coffee or red wine and anecdotes were exchanged but they never talked about architecture.

Aalto never developed his ideas in dialogue, by exchanging ideas with others, he needed to be alone, to concentrate in seclusion. The short route between his house and the studio was of considerable importance for his creative process. "He thought while walking," Nava is completely convinced. Like the staff in the archive in Jyväskylä he emphasises that nature and above all the trees Aalto loved so much were central sources of inspiration for him. "He had a fantastic intuition to see the house on the ground, the house it is part of nature. Nature inspired him, all its developed forms, Finnish nature, the Finnish lakes, islands and rocks, the woods, the way wood developed, he hated symmetry, that was a big taboo, everything was asymmetrical." When drawing up competition entries or at times when they were working on many different commissions simultaneously, additional desks were brought into Aalto's personal work area, which deeply irritated him.

He often took sketches home with him, Georg Schwalm-Theiss recalls from his time as an intern in Aalto's office. "He sat in a restaurant downtown. He would work on paper from the restaurant and bring it back to the office," says Nava invoking the mythical sketch on the paper napkin. In the memories from those days these napkin sketches play just as important a role as the ones made on the plain backs of the packages of Aalto's favourite cigarettes "Klubi 77 Klubb," as Marja-Liisa Hänninen remarks.

ALVAR AALTO FREQUENTLY MADE FIRST SKETCHES ON THE PLAIN BACKS
OF HIS FAVOURITE CIGARETTES, THE KLUBI 77 KLUBB.
SKIZZE UNIVERSITY OF TECHNOLOGY, OTANIEMI 1949–1974
ARCHIVES OF THE ALVAR AALTO MUSEUM, JYVÄSKYLÄ

VEZIO NAVA

"He sketched intuitively."

"He sketched intuitively," Nava says about the maestro or "boss," who sat at his large, light brown wooden desk covered with thin white plastic with his back to the window. Every morning the secretary laid out several layers of sketch paper cut to a length of 30 cm. "His drawing table had to be tidy. Everything had to be in order. He even arranged his pencils in order of length before beginning to draw," Michele Merckling recounts in "Studio Aalto," a half-hour-long documentary film made in 2005 by the Alvar Aalto Museum

Alongside the 6B the other most important tool was the Finnish sketch paper, tervakoski luonnospaperi, which, according to Vezio Nava, is the best in the world because it is so thin. In the drawing studio directly beside the foot of the stairs there are many rolls of paper lying on the plan chest, some in their original packaging. "The sketches of Aalto, for us they were incredibly complete, even if they were done with a trembling hand. When you started to make the drawing from the sketches, there wasn't anything you could not find in the sketches. Many times the sketches and the drawings they go together, the first sketch, the scale drawing, the sketch on the scale drawing, another scale drawing, many times he asked for the scale drawing to work on," Vezio Nava recalls, explaining the sequence of the creative process. "You have to understand Aalto's strong personality. His manner was incredibly infectious, a strong influence. Two or three people in the office even started to sketch the same way as he did." Marja-Liisa Hänninen in the archive in Jyväskylä confirms this, and explains that today it is impossible to say with certainty which sketches were made by Aalto and which by long-term

ELISSA AALTO ON ALVAR AALTO'S WORKING PRACTICE

"He didn't particularly like the working drawing stage. Details however were terribly important — he sketched them."

PHOTOS CLOCKWISE: MÄKINEN EINO, ALVAR AALTO SÄÄTIÖ; MOSSO LEONARDO, ALVAR AALTO SÄÄTIÖ; BERGSTRÖM STIG, ALVAR AALTO SÄÄTIÖ; HOLMA MAIJA AAM, ALVAR AALTO SÄÄTIÖ

members of staff. Given the 500 to 5,000 sketches and plans made for each project it is also hardly possible to reconstruct in detail the chronology of the development processes. On some sketches there are even children's drawings, shopping lists or notes about completely different projects.

"In the office we worked in a very practical way, just using our hands and sketching and drawing. We could not ask him or press him to do something, we just waited. I saw the sketches on his table, he would never have come to me to tell me. His way of work was very elastic. When he talked to you, he put some doubt into your mind, but he was not telling you what to do." Development took place through examination using the medium of the drawing. "You learned here that you never get it right the first time. You had to draw it over and over again," Eric Adlercreutz recalls in the "Studio Aalto" film. In 1958 Aalto wrote in the January/ February issue of Arkkitehti magazine: "The Creator created paper to draw architecture on. Everything else is, at least as far as I see it, a misuse of paper."

REFERENCES

Blomstedt, Anssi (2005) Studio Aalto, Film 31 min, The Alvar Aalto Museum, 2005
Fleig, Karl (1995) Die Arbeit im Atelier, in: Alar Aalto: Volume II, 1963–1970, Basel, 9–11
Paaterno, Kristiina (Ed.) (1993) The Line: Original Drawings from the Alvar Aalto Archive, trans. Hildi Hawkins, Helsinki

SKETCHES UNIVERSITY OF TECHNOLOGY, OTANIEMI 1949–1974
ARCHIVES OF THE ALVAR AALTO MUSEUM, JYVÄSKYLÄ

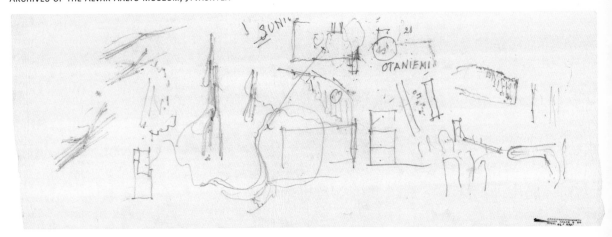

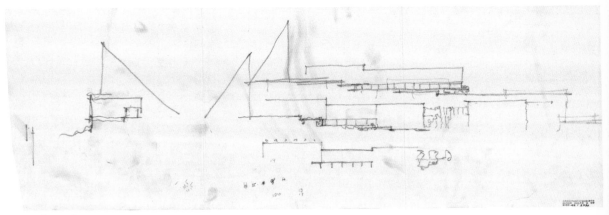

ELISSA AALTO

"His whole approach was that the architect could change his mind during construction, make changes."

FIGURES: ALVAR AALTO SÄÄTIÖ

A small socialist experiment

Lina Bo Bardi 1914–1992

Instituto Lina Bo e P. M. Bardi
Rua Bandeirante Sampaio Soares,
420, Morumbi
São Paulo, Brazil

Research in the Instituto Lina Bo e P. M. Bardi in August 2007
photography, discussions with Marcelo Suzuki
& Text: Elke Krasny

If you saw two or three construction workers' hard hats hanging on the wall then you knew immediately that this was the studio of Lina Bo Bardi, says Marcelo Suzuki, who worked for Bo Bardi from 1981 to her death in 1992. But Suzuki warns one should not imagine anything like a conventional architect's office with a secretary to answer the phone and to deal with the bank business.

From 1977 to 1986 Lina Bo Bardi worked on a project in the factory grounds of the steel fibre producers Mauser & Cia Ltda that included new construction as well as conversion work to turn the site into what is today the SESC Fábrica da Pompéia leisure and culture facility in São Paulo. For nine years she had her office in a container unit directly on the construction site. "Una casinha," a little house, is how Suzuki describes the studio on the building site. Bo Bardi's practice of architecture was just as close to the skills of building construction as it was to the poetry of the imagination. In her practice she wanted to demonstrate the different way in which she understood architecture that related to the medieval system of masons' lodges or to Antoni Gaudí. Her last studio was also a kind of "lodge," a log cabin in her own garden that opened directly onto rampantly luxurious vegetation in every imaginable shade of green.

The open fireplace in the Glass House, erected in 1951 and today the home of the Instituto Lina Bo e P.M. Bardi, played a central role in all the design processes. Here the three or four members of staff met with "Dona Lisa," as she was respectfully known, and discussed things. SESC Pompéia also has a huge fireplace in the open reading room cum lounge. "Talk, talk, talk," Suzuki recalls. Sketches were made with whatever happened to be at hand, at times even with a forefinger moistened with spittle and some cigarette ash. They only worked on one project at a time, never on several simultaneously.

"I can not imagine Lina with an enormous group or a big office. She wanted to form a group, like a co-operation. But everyone also needs his individual work. That is what she always said." Lina brought reference material from the library. This could take the form of a poem by Goethe or illustrations of Japanese children taking a walk in a park. She never brought books specifically about architecture with her. "She showed us something like a reference. An image of the Piazza Navona to explain why something was built that way or the hand-woven Brazilian baskets she collected to show us that all the cultures have something modern, a modern way of producing something we can find out about."

For Lina Bo Bardi, who left Italy with her husband Pietro Maria Bardi in 1946 after the Second World War and took Brazilian citizenship in 1951, Brazil was not just a second home;

MARCELO SUZUKI

"We don't have an office with a secretary to answer the telephone or to go to the bank because we are another kind of architect."

she proclaimed: "Brazil is twice my country." (BO BARDI: NO DATE) At a time when the architecture public was fascinated by the modernist architectural movement in Brazil, Lina Bo Bardi travelled through the undeveloped northeast, the Sertão, a dry and impoverished region. She called her exploration an "anthropological quest." (BO BARDI: 1976) She began to collect goods that formed part of the regional culture and researched domestic handcraft and local building traditions. This examination of the "popular civilisation" then became the decisive inspiration for her work and for the design process with her staff. She attempted to foster an appreciation of this popular culture, an interest in "the cultural currents of the Brazilian people" (IBID. BO BARDI: 1976). In her eyes, which, as she was an immigrant, were perhaps better able to discern the specific culture of her new home, the juxtaposing of high and low-tech was decisive. She endeavoured to integrate this quality in her practice of architecture. The workers who developed the structural solution for the water tower of SESC by means of a number of proto-types but without a predetermined plan were workers from Sertão who had moved home within Brazil and whose skill as craftsmen had so impressed Lina Bo Bardi during her travels.

Lina Bo Bardi, who had joined the illegal Communist Party in Italy during the Second World War, categorically refused to design demonstratively impressive buildings for banks or

MARCELO SUZUKI

"She sketched with whatever you can think of, even using her finger and ash from the ash tray."

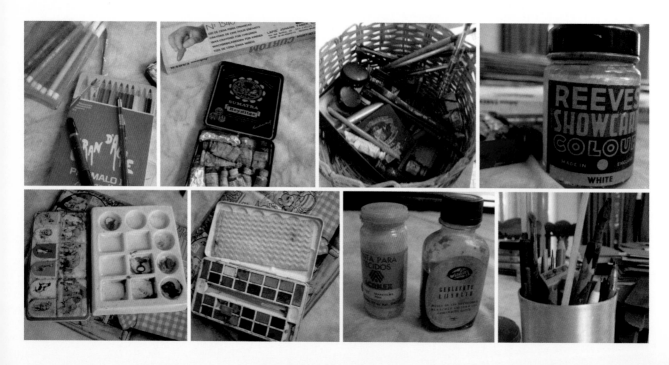

luxury houses for private clients, and she equally emphatically rejected technical plans as a means of communication with craftsmen and construction workers. The lines of the plans on her colourful drawings, which she embellished with texts, were drawn by her staff. Today the desk with a cast-iron base and glass top that Lina Bo Bardi imported from Italy stands in the architecture studio cum apartment of Marcelo Suzuki, who prepared many of the basic drawings for her. She kept numerous felt pens, coloured pencils, watercolours, turpentine and innumerable brushes in baskets she collected. Lina Bo Bardi's typical, strongly expressive drawings do not comply with the standardised norms of architectural plans. In her watercolour sketches she combined illustrative depiction, technical details and short descriptions. She was inspired by the Renaissance tradition of architectural symbols.

"Lina had a very particular way of designing, because she had a great interest in popular culture, in the pattern of life in different civilizations. She took a specific look at Africa, at Japan, at Brazil. In Brazil we have so many different cultures. She attempted to open our eyes to this, to make us see like she did." She made great demands on culture as the production of a community rather than the lofty product of an elite or a remote museological form of representation. In the MASP, the Museu de Arte de São Paulo, which she designed and her

TODAY LINA BO BARDI'S DESK STANDS IN THE
STUDIO CUM APARTMENT OF MARCELO SUZUKI

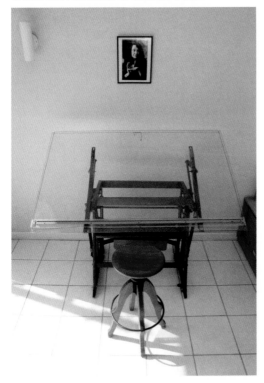

MARCELO SUZUKI

"Lina's desk was imported from Italy.
She gave me the desk because I did the base
for many of her drawings."

husband directed, she initiated a school, taught design classes and produced exhibitions. She also maintained her connection with the SESC Pompéia after its completion and designed exhibitions there such as "Design no Brasil: historia e realidade" (Design in Brazil: History and Reality) 1982 or "Mil brinquedos para a crianca brasileira" (A Thousand Toys for the Brazilian Child) in 1983. This preserving the connection to her own work long after the construction had been completed is a characteristic that Marcelo Suzuki regards as gender-specific: "Only women can stay with their works, like with children. It was a mother-child-relation she had with her works."

REFERENCE
Bardi, Lina (1976) Planejamento Ambiental (Environmental Planning), in Malasartes no 2.
www.institutobardi.com.br/

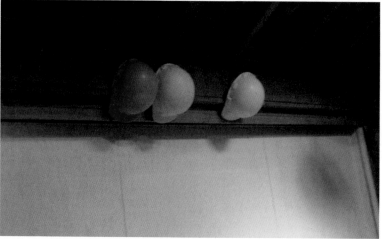

MARCELO SUZUKI

"We sat around her fireplace and talked."

PHOTOS: INSTITUTO LINA BO E P.M. BARDI, ELKE KRASNY

SKETCHES, SESC (SOCIAL SERVICE FOR COMMERCE)
POMPÉIA, SÃO PAULO, 1977–1986

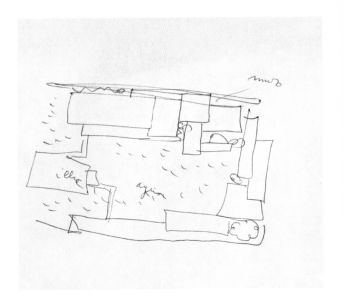

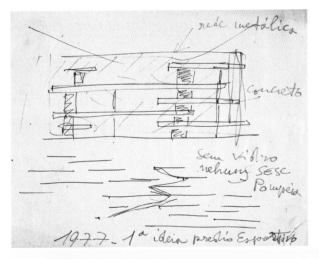

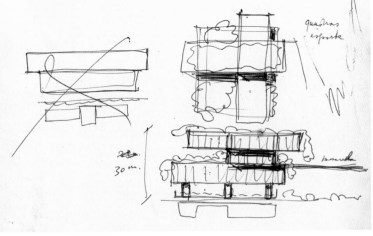

FIGURES: INSTITUTO LINA BO E P.M. BARDI

MARCELO SUZUKI

"She never showed us books on architecture."

NOTES, SESC POMPÉIA, SÃO PAULO, 1977–1986

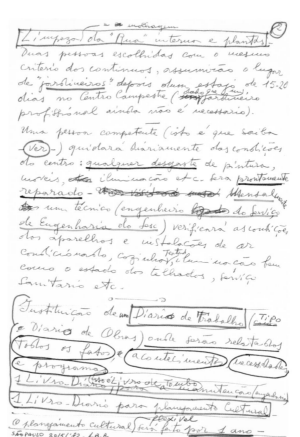

MARCELO SUZUKI

"She showed us objects, for example baskets, she had bought in the Northeast of Brazil."

DIAGRAMME, SESC POMPÉIA, SÃO PAULO, 1977–1986

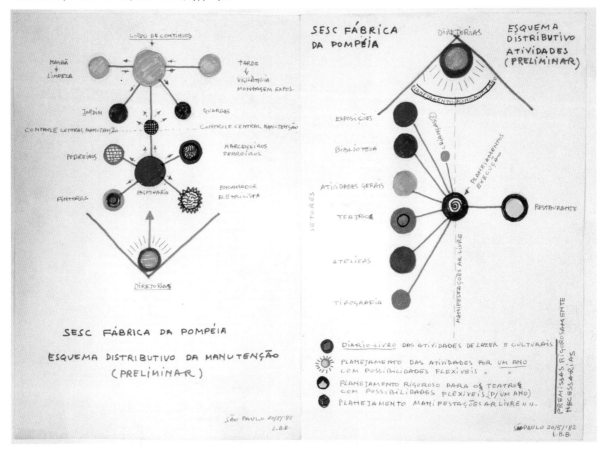

DESIGN, FOUR GYMNASIUMS SPRING, AUTUMN, WINTER AND SUMMER, SESC POMPÉIA, SÃO PAULO, 1977–1986

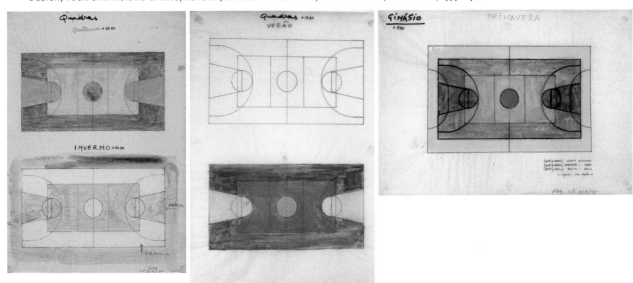

MARCELO SUZUKI

"She opened our eyes to see."

As precise as possible

Atelier Bow-Wow

8-79 Suga-cho
Shinjuku-ku
Tokio
Japan

Field research in the studio in August 2007
photography, interviews and conversations
with Momoyo Kaijima, Yoshiharu Tsukamoto,
staff members and interns & text: Elke Krasny

Extreme precision and a sophisticated handling of proportion and scale characterise the way in which Atelier Bow-Wow works. After several changes of location this practice has now arrived at the ideal combination of living and working. "It's always good to use a building all around the clock," says Yoshiharu Tsukamoto. Standing on a typical Tokyo site connected to the road by a narrow access strip, the studio cum dwelling house they designed is also a kind of three-dimensional visiting card. "Client meeting in ten minutes, please sweep the floor." Discussions with clients are held at the large conference table. Visual connections between the different levels allow visitors an insight into the entire studio. The model building table and computer workstations are at lower ground level, while further workstations, including those of Momoyo Kaijima and Yoshiharu Tsukamoto, lie one split-level above the entrance. Atelier Bow-Wow specialise in "global detached houses," a description they coined for single-family houses specially tailored to the shortage of space in Tokyo. Holding the model in hand they discuss all the details with the client, and any changes that are required are entered manually immediately in the plans lying on the table.

"The clients want a lot of things. So many functions and so little space," Momoyo Kaijima analyses the main challenge for which a tailor-made solution has to be found in each case. "We are always on a tight schedule, discussion needs to be short, every two weeks we meet with the client. On average a detached house takes three months. We do sketches, perspectives and views, the client is not a professional."

They deal with twenty different projects at any one time, each of the six employees working on between three and five projects. The staff studied either under Yoshiharu Tsukamoto, who teaches at the Tokyo Institute of Technology, or under Momoyo Kaijima, who teaches at Tskuba University. Interns, most of them from Europe, work for between two weeks and a maximum of six months in the studio. These jobs are much sought-after.

"There is one person who is in charge and one collaborator. They have to rush, there is a lot of work to do. I always talk with my staff and suggest the directions." A team meeting is held every Monday. Plans and models are spread out on the large table, the staff talk about day-to-day experiences. The second work area of this studio, urban research carried out primarily with the help of students, and micro public spaces at the various art biennales are closely related to the development of the detached houses.

On the day they start work in the studio all new staff members are given a tour of the entire building. There is only one entrance, where shoes are taken off and left on a white

MOMOYO KAIJIMA

"We make a surrounding model of the topography. With the model we check the design process, spatially."

sheepskin. The two work levels are followed by a kitchen and living area with a balcony. Models stand on a table at the staircase landing and have already spread into the living room also. The fourth floor containing the bedrooms and bathroom is private. On the roof garden, which is open to everyone during studio parties, plants are grown in small wooden troughs. "Everyday life is a very good source, the city itself, people's behaviour, building behaviour, natural elements' behaviour, are very inspiring, trees and masks are very good inspiration."

"The beginning is imagining the scenario. We try to make a scenario by collecting information. For a small house we spend one hour on site, for a bigger project half a day." The building site is photographed, the photos mounted to make a panorama. Ideas are developed jointly through the discussion process. "Brainstorming is important. The most important thing to do is to find out what the architectural problem is. The problem finding, or I should say finding out the contradiction, is the most important thing. Discussing is very important, but then I need time to think alone," says Yoshiharu Tsukamoto. Models are built and plans are drawn on the basis of rough sketches. Every change made to the design is

YOSHIHARU TSUKAMOTO

"The social relationships are changed by the computer. For me architecture is very related to the social form. The computer is not just a question inside architecture. The impact of the computer on society may change architecture."

examined in a new model. First of all the overall volumes are examined, then the interior of the house and its exact proportions are worked out. Site visits are made again during the development process to determine the exact positioning of the openings.

"I like very much to bring different types of conditions into a single physical entity. This room has a very big window," Tsukamoto points to his living room window. "This room is exposed to different generations of houses in the urban landscape. We can position ourselves in the history of a place." In the studio one notices how the perception of space can be altered by leaps in scale. "We gave more space to the staircase. In many cases the staircase is just the minimum required. Changing the dimensions is a reaction to the lack of the space." The important thing is the relationship between volume and proportion. They build models in all imaginable scales — 1:100, 1:50, 1:30.

"In the 1990s model building became very common amongst good architects in Japan. All our models are to scale, scientific and precise. We are as precise as possible; we work to scale and take very, very great care with the proportions. Basically we build 50 to 60 models

T-HOUSE IN MANAZARU, KANAGAWA, COMPLETION AUTUMN 2008

T-HOUSE, FIRST SKETCH, 2008

YOSHIHARU TSUKAMOTO

"All our models are to scale and scientific and precise. We are as precise as possible."

per project. But now I have more literacy of the architectural language, I could think about reducing the amount of models built per project." The models are made of styrofoam and cardboard and high precision Japanese cutters and non-drip American glue are used to build them.

"Pencil and paper, foam and cardboard models and the computer," Yoshiharu Tsukamoto lists his architectural tools. Propelling pencils, thin fineliners and an entire wall with diverse model building tools including protective masks, and sprays as well as CAD enjoy equal status. CAD drawing is largely the domain of the staff. "In our design there are very few repetitions, so for us the computer has only a rare potential. There is more digital stock in other architects' practices. In fact I am not so advanced as to find any clues between the reality of my architec-

YOSHIHARU TSUKAMOTO
"Every day life is a very good source, the city itself, people's behaviour, buildings' behaviour, natural elements' behaviour, are very inspiring, trees and masks are very good."

ture and those kinds of technologies with the computer. The social relationships are changed by the computer. For me architecture is related to the social form. The computer is not just a question inside architecture. The impact of the computer on society may change architecture, but I don't know yet how to make this a context for my design."

T-HOUSE, COMPLETION AUTUMN 2008

YOSHIHARU TSUKAMOTO

"We try to make a scenario by collecting information. For a small house we spend one hour on site. For a bigger project we spend half a day."

Primarily with words

Hermann Czech

SINGERSTRASSE 26A
VIENNA
AUSTRIA

FIELD RESEARCH IN THE STUDIO IN 2007 AND JUNE 2008
PHOTOGRAPHY AND CONVERSATIONS WITH
HERMANN CZECH & TEXT: ELKE KRASNY

"At the beginning I don't really have much in the way of ideas, perhaps some vague notion of structure, an approach to a spatial concept." Hermann Czech has no specific rituals that he uses when starting work. "On the first page of his cash registers my father always wrote 'with God.' I don't use rituals of that kind." Projects begin by someone asking him a question which leads to "thinking over something and looking at it. There are no uninteresting commissions but there are commissions that don't cover the costs they involve."

Analysis of the site is essential. "Ideally, you should spend time there during different seasons of the year. The more often you go there, the better, but it's not the length of time spent there that counts but the repetition. If I can choose, I prefer to visit a place twice for ten minutes than once for twenty minutes. The site is documented. I have always taken photos, something that used to be far more tedious." Digital photographs are printed out and fetched, "when I can't remember something or am looking for information." Sometimes drawings are made on the photos. "A short while ago I acted as consultant for somebody, and we drew on the photos, rendered them using Photoshop. I had just thought beforehand: for me the staff are a means, as I can't do anything on the computer. I can't use programmes like Photoshop at all. It's not the computer that's an important tool but staff who are understanding."

Generally the office has a staff of between four and five, several of them work on different projects at the same time and they are informed about everything from the very start, as otherwise explaining things would be too time-consuming. A number of them have been working in the office for ten years or more. Hermann Czech communicates with them "primarily by talking, but sometimes by drawing." The more the staff members adapt to the process, the better they know what to ask. "Whom an idea comes from has nothing to do with its value. But I make the decisions."

The computer arrived in 2000, introduced by a staff member who brought her computer with her to the office to work on. "The way of working hasn't consciously changed as a result of the computer. I make hardly any drawings that are intended as a basis for implementation. And I don't make any at all with the computer. But this isn't a change, as I didn't draw anything previously either." In much the same way as he draws little, Hermann Czech also builds few models. "I'm not a good model maker myself but in the office we do make a few." When they have fulfilled their purpose the working models are thrown away. As regards sketches, too, Czech does not attach any importance to the original, because the basic means of reproduction today is digital.

HERMANN CZECH

"I don't read easily."

During the conversation Hermann Czech repeatedly stands up to go and look for something that can demonstrate the way he works. He returns to the room with a spatial sketch of his café (that no longer exists) in the Museum of Applied Art, the MAK in Vienna. "This was a spatial sketch for the MAK, it is on an A4 sheet made using a thick felt pen. Everything is included but it is very schematic, nobody can understand it unless it is explained to them. The sketch is not a means of discovering an idea, but a record of decisions. I'm not someone who invents forms or composes concepts in my mind, but someone who lives from the many existing preconditions." The design process is not shaped by the search for form but by the "temporal sequence of decisions. It is really true that you differentiate between things you have to decide about immediately and those you don't have to decide about. In particular there are often administrative reasons why you can't decide something and then you see to it that this area is separated and you do something that means this area can be left open. I don't like to leaving decisions open, but either there are things where one doesn't know the solution or things where you don't have the proper basis on which to make a decision."

His constantly growing library is an ever-present tool. On each of our visits Czech emphasises that the room has reached the limits of its load-bearing capacity. You reach his

HERMANN CZECH

"I explain myself using historical examples."

studio by climbing an angled staircase connecting two buildings and have to walk up six floors — there is no elevator. In the 19th century the building housed the State Printing Office. The short end of the building was opened up by making windows that look towards St. Stephen's Cathedral. The walls to the meeting room are formed by glazed book shelves, which he designed himself, that can be locked. "I only read a fraction of what I have collected here. Often I put a marker in a book where I think to myself: I really must read that some time. But it can also happen that I take down a book and say to myself: that's a theme which I should look at and then I find that I have already underlined or highlighted everything. I have read the whole thing but have no idea about it any more," he says with a laugh. Book-marks inserted in the books, often in the form of a copied or enlarged detail, are traces of this continuous searching. "I don't read easily. I find it difficult to concentrate."

On the meeting room table only a small area remains free, books are stacked to the left and right of it, between them lies a roll of tracing paper, at the edge there is a cup containing pencils. An important tool is "a pencil with an eraser at the end that works properly. In the HB range. The eraser is important, so that you can change things immediately." No less important is the metal cap at the other end. "These sleeves are now available again. For decades you couldn't buy them. They are important because otherwise you can't stick the pencil into your breast pocket." When he is on the move he generally has a small notebook with him, "generally squared paper, with small squares."

HERMANN CZECH

"I'm not someone who invents forms or composes concepts in my mind, but someone who lives from the many existing preconditions."

"I search for solutions" says Hermann Czech. The statement can be understood both figuratively and literally. But he has made relatively few architecture journeys. "I have seen too little, but what I have seen has a productive context." His search sets him in motion, motivates him to look through his books or his extensive collection of slides for references from the history of architecture. "Very often I introduce examples, also at the design phase; I bring along a historic detail and say: 'something analogous in the figurative sense, that's the direction I want to go in.' I explain myself using historical examples." Completed buildings are also examined. "This is not my own speciality. There are, however, people who never bother to do this. In earlier days I always had a measuring tape with me but not any longer, now I have my mobile phone and the car keys. But I miss it, I used always to measure steps. I have an entire collection of stairs I have measured. A stairs is a very subtle instrument." Although architecture is a tool, the issue is not the "historic contexts" but the potential to activate a problem that has already been solved in the past for use in a current situation seen as similar. "Generally using specific instances, along the line 'he had a similar problem or an analogous one and this is how he solved it.'" In "repetition or quotation, or whatever you want to call it" the solution is looked at in terms of its "usability". "Then we check it." The way in which the solutions discovered or selected are handled involves a considerable degree of "wit" and irony.

HOTEL MESSE WIEN
Picture selection and text: Hermann Czech

The urban figure of this curved and inclined building exploits the boundaries of the site; as a result it defines the surrounding street spaces in much the same way as a continuous development.

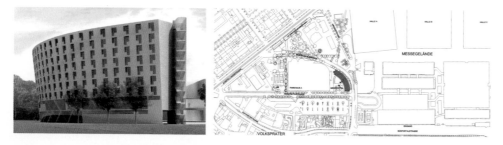

Changes of mind on the part of the investor and operator about how the building would be used emerged after the competition, initially leading to a certain inflation of the building's form and with it a loss of clarity. At this phase it is pointless to try to stop this development; you have to trust that it will later be possible to clarify the design again and make it more precise. Nonetheless the zoning application of the project was based on the design with the maximum volume.

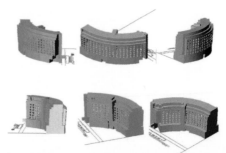

The building is tilted by about 3.6°. The distinctive element of the inclined walls, just like the curving of the building, is noticeable also in the interior – for instance in the corridors.

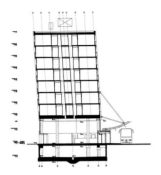 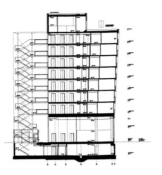 

RENDERING: WOLGANG BEYER

Usually on renderings you can "see everything"; except what really will be done. Unlike the usual strategy the simulation (Wolfgang Beyer, also the "green" one of the competition entry) shows the actual current state of the design, so that at a late stage it shows the building in a deceptively realistic way.

PHOTO: VALENTIN SCHEINOST

Towards the entrance to the trade fair the fronts of service rooms become particularly prominent. The intention here is, rather than frustrating those who have just noticed the hotel building volume by presenting them, as they approach, with a dead ground floor zone, to instead unconsciously engage their interest, until finally the foyer spaces enter their field of vision.

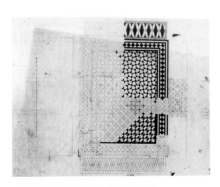

The black and white pattern used here is a design by Leo von Klenze (dating from around 1825, for the floor of a room in the Glyptothek in Munich). Klenze probably arrived at this unsettling effect by chance; it is hard to explain in terms of the psychology of perception how this effect is created using only this relatively simple geometry (on this account it appears almost impossible to intensify this effect). This puzzling pattern is something one remembers when one returns here, and also makes vandalisation (by graffiti or whatever) less likely.

Plain aluminium is employed on this facade as a cladding material that is capable of weathering. Experts warn that this surface could weather "unattractively". For this reason the plain areas alternate with anthracite-coloured, coated areas that interrupt them and as a result "frame" them. Even if certain areas do weather in an aesthetically unsatisfactory way, they are integrated in an overall image by the conscious presentation of the design intention.
The width of the horizontal strips is determined by the width of a sheet of the material. These dimensions overlap with the floor height (ca. 5:7).

The real or symbolised layering of masonry courses of a wall is to be found in historic examples.

The areas used by the public and the guests are transparent and allow a view through the volume of the building. Parts of this foyer zone are double-height (something normally not possible in this category). The inclined columns (visible also from outside) provide the structural transition between the grid of the underground garage and that of the walls on the bedroom floor levels. Originally designed as Y-shaped, in the first design their upper end marked the otherwise invisible position of the structural ceiling. This perspective is not a rendering, but a graphic work in its own right (albeit produced with the computer).

PHOTO: MARGHERITA SPILUTTINI

This type of armchair made familiar by Le Corbusier is alienated by a grip suited to the shape of the hand which is a help in getting up out of the chair – Le Corbusier's 'Grand confort' is here "confronted" with current requirements for the aged or disabled. (The Cassina company is currently making this design the subject of a copyright lawsuit).

Other chair designs that refer to quoted models in a way that reflects the (temporal) distance:

(1)   *(2)*   *(3)*

(1) 1961 (Restaurant Ballhaus, with Wolfgang Mistelbauer and Reinald Nohal): reconstruction of a chair design dating from the 1930s, upholstered with a newly woven textile based on a (modified) design from 1907 (in the room is a reprint of a wallpaper from 1913) – all designs by Josef Hoffmann, who would never have combined them in this way.

(2) 1984 (Restaurant in Palais Schwarzenberg): chair design based on a model from the early 19th century, when our notion of what makes a comfortable chair originated.

(3) 1993 (initially MAK-Café, now serially manufactured by Thonet Vienna): modification of what was for a long time the most inexpensive Thonet model (probably from the 1930s); to meet changes in the way we sit today this model has a somewhat wider and more inclined chair back.

PHOTOS (1) AND (2): HARALD SCHÖNFELLINGER

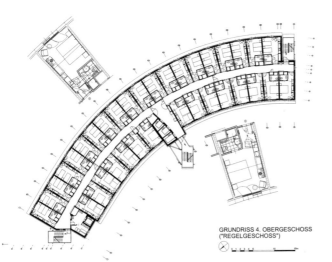

The radial layout produces different room types on either side of the corridor. Further differences result from the choice between shower or bathtub (Japanese tourists, for example, insist on bathtubs), the occasional demand for additional beds, some rooms for disabled persons and, finally, there are also differences caused by different radii along the building, which additionally, due to the incline of the building, increase from floor to floor by 17 cm. (Fortunately there are not quite 243 different types for the 243 bedrooms). The tapering shape of the bedrooms is handled in the area of the door and the mirror by further angles that open up the space.

GRUNDRISS 4. OBERGESCHOSS
("REGELGESCHOSS")

As hotel room closets are generally far too voluminous and only part of them is used, here they are only 150 cm high, which is tall enough to hang up clothes in, if nothing is kept below the clothes. This low height also improves the view into the room.

right: The architect's own closet as an example.

The disadvantage of the nearby parking deck is mitigated by giving this western side of the hotel a representative, public character, so that it forms a plaza including the driveway. The tilt of the building helps underline the upgrading of this concave plaza front.

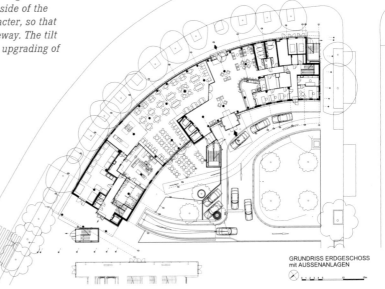

GRUNDRISS ERDGESCHOSS
mit AUSSENANLAGEN

PHOTOS: MARGHERITA SPILUTTINI

COLLABORATORS: ANNA-MARIJA DUFILS-MENIGA, ANDREAS MIELING, THOMAS ROTH, VALENTIN SCHEINOST, GEORG ÜBELHÖR; STRUCTURAL AND MECHANICAL SERVICES CONSULTANT, QUANTITY SURVEYOR: ATP ACHAMMER — TRITTHART & PARTNER; INVESTOR: UNIVERSALE INTERNATIONAL; OPERATOR: AUSTRIA TREND HOTELS & RESORTS

Almost anything can be a tool

Diller Scofidio + Renfro

601 West 26 Street #1815
New York
USA

Field research in the studio in January 2007
photography, discussions with
Elizabeth Diller, Partner Charles Renfro,
staff members and interns, text: Gudrun Hausegger

"It's hard to articulate very clearly what the process is, because the work is so varied and it has happened over the course of pre-computer and post-computer. I think more than almost any other studio the projects are so extremely varied that we kind of customize methodologies to each project. We are a research-based studio, and even if it is a client-driven project, we always start out with research," says Elizabeth Diller, who together with Ricardo Scofidio set up Diller + Scofidio in New York in 1979. In 2004 Charles Renfro — who had worked in the practice since 1997 — became a partner and the name of the office was changed to Diller Scofidio + Renfro.

Since the office was first set up the work of this team has transcended the boundaries between the disciplines of architecture, visual and performing arts, has carried out dance projects, multi-media art installations and investigated innovative media. They collaborate with artists from very different areas such as dance, theatre and new technologies. "We have spent our careers trying to break down disciplinary boundaries," says Elizabeth Diller. Their office is made up exclusively of architects who feel attracted by the interdisciplinary direction of the work. When needed people with a different professional background are brought in at short notice. "At the moment there is a seamster working in the model shop who is helping us evolve the shaping of a particular bag, because we are developing a light design for Swarovski. So we hired somebody that just distinctly is able to help us pattern and sew. We turn architecture around. This is, because we come from the discipline of architecture as opposed to hiring people from other disciplines. We don't have a need for that, because we already think in space and gravity as unusual architects. That comes from our perverse way of thinking about architecture," Diller explains.

The design process operates non-hierarchically: the three partners and the particular design team discuss ideas and possibilities and develop them together. After this the team continues the work, modifies it and receives support in the form of further regular discussions. During the design phase all three partners are involved in the process to equal extents, initially the responsibilities are not distributed and it is only from a certain point onwards that one or other of the partners take on the further supervision of the project.

The research phase, too, is non-hierarchical. There is no separate research department, all the members of the project team take part in the research process, and discuss the different areas of competence. These phases take up considerable amounts of time, one or two years for a project is nothing unusual, the outcome of the research always remains

ELIZABETH DILLER

"When one goes directly to computing then you are actually not thinking. I don't like sketching, just because it is a nostalgia about the hand. It's really about thinking fast."

unpredictable. "There are always inventions that are created for projects. Research is predisposed to experimental work. Like with the Blur Building for the Swiss Expo 2002 we wanted to make a building out of water. But is there something like a specialist for fog, a fog engineer? And a lot of our work has to do with producing effects, so we often need to transform existing technologies and come up with materials that have never been used in these ways," explains Elizabeth Diller. "A lot of our research is hands-on-research — to try physically to make something, to make it over and over again. Sometimes to test it at its final 1:1 scale," Charles Renfro adds.

This unorthodox design process requires the unconventional use of instruments. Elizabeth Diller: "We see almost anything as a potential tool to help us think. The real challenge lies in the circumstances themselves, because sometimes circumstances produce the needs to invent a new tool. Sometimes the fact that there is a tool allows you to think about things you have never thought about before. But we are not obsessed with the tools. The tools are whatever we can use."

In their work Diller Scofidio + Renfro consistently investigate themes such as the culture of perception, the choreography of spaces and the relationship between new technologies and new architecture. "We are interested in technology and architecture in all sorts of ways — going beyond the convention of smart architecture, the IQ of architecture in a kind of complex way," says Elizabeth Diller. The path from research to practice is never a linear one. They consistently overstep boundaries and contravene conventions. "The quality of our work mostly comes from the desire to think through something that has not existed before. I mean that in a certain sense — we are not interested in novelties just for the sake of novelties," Diller adds.

"We have spent our careers in trying to break down the disciplinary boundaries. We can say what we do, but we cannot say that architecture is one thing or the other. For us it is really about space, about defining space in relationship to engagement, sites and activities. Architecture is all about defining space, because space is there, before you get there."

Despite their fascination with new technologies the computer does not have overriding importance for Diller Scofidio + Renfro, which is to say it is not a mandatory design tool: "I don't like to say old-fashioned or new. It is more — these are all tools and these are all available. For me the discrepancy when one goes directly to computing is that you are actually not thinking. I don't just like sketching because of nostalgia about the hand. It is really about thinking fast, because you can test all sorts of complex relations very, very quickly. It is just a way for architects and people in visual arts to think," says Elizabeth Diller, adopting a clear position.

For over 20 years they worked in a two-storey office that was also Elizabeth Diller and Ricardo Scofidio's apartment. The space was cramped, there was a lack of room for discussions with clients or for a model-building workshop. At the end of 2006 they moved to a loft in Chelsea where 40 people of different international backgrounds now work. There is a large model workshop in the basement. Discussing the location of their new office in New York Charles Renfro explains: "Where we are located in the city is a really interesting representation of what the office stands for in the world. We are in Manhattan, but we are on the very edge. There is a visual connection, but also a critical distance. It was a choice that we had to make whether to be inserted in the city or on the edge." And they chose a location that is both central and marginal.

ALICE TULLY HALL, NEW YORK,
DIFFERENT STAGES OF THE DESIGN PROCESS

ELIZABETH DILLER

"We are not obsessed by computing technologies. We see almost anything as a potential tool to help us think. But the real challenge is in the circumstances themselves, because sometimes circumstances produce the need to invent a new tool, or sometimes, the fact that there is a tool allows you to think about things you have never thought about before. But we are not obsessed without tools."

Tools have another side

Edge Design Institute

Suite 1604, Eastern Harbour Centre
28 Hoi Chak Street, Quarry Bay
Hong Kong

Field research in the office in July 2007
photography, discussions with Gary Chang, staff and
clients & text: Elke Krasny

"Tools have another life, a multiple personality," says Gary Chang, who has headed the Edge Design Institute in Hong-Kong (which he founded) since 1994. Mobile working is part of his everyday life; he spends 120 nights of the year in hotels. "Tools should be multipurpose," adds the nomadic worker Chang as he rummages through his leather backpack for suitable objects to demonstrate his point. "But at the moment there is no single tool to work on everything. It sounds good to say: it is just my laptop and me and we can work anywhere, but the computer is only one aspect. I don't use the computer too much. I like to be in control of tools. I don't want to be technology dominated. I couldn't narrow it down to one tool, even though that sounds good for mobility. I still carry a sketchbook. I have a special addiction to small books. Even when I travel I carry them with me."

Chang doesn't use his i-Pod to listen to music but to store and show images. His central concerns here are multi-functionality and the ability to transform the images. This approach is consistently developed in the way he uses tools, in the design of his own office, in the creative processes as well as in the production of architecture. "The recurring theme of our office is transformation." The acceleration of work processes is just as important as the convertibility of space. "We develop a methodology of fast track design." To survive in Hong Kong — and perhaps even more so in mainland China — "instant design" is essential. Nonetheless, as its name suggests, the Edge Design Institute attempts to connect accelerated productivity with research "Before starting a new project, we always go to the site. This is a must. We mostly document the site photographically sometimes we do videos. But we also talk to people, not just the client; we try to find out what is happening in the surroundings. This cannot be done fast track. We might know Hong Kong very well, but that doesn't mean we have all the information. Things are very fragile. Hong Kong is a very rapidly changing city. We have to research and actively gather information."

To generate ideas quickly unusual means are employed: "In terms of speed Lego blocks are a very good tool to work with. I can do a model in three minutes. If you are brainstorming and you want to explain the idea you don't have to focus on the scale so much. They are extremely good for conceptual models." As a child Chang got his first Lego pieces in 1969, not the original ones but copies made in Japan. Four years ago, when the office moved to a new location, Chang bought an enormous amount of Lego pieces that now lie on a long, narrow table waiting to be used. "I feel like a professor in the office. We often start with a brainstorming. We don't need to go to the meeting room. The organization of the office

GARY CHANG

"We develop a methodology of fast track design."

makes it suitable for brainstorming everywhere. It is very productive and efficient, like an informal in-house seminar. A lot of things are fixed on the first day."

The office works on 25 to 30 projects at the same time. "We don't split up into rigid teams, as a result the office can remain organic. When something is really urgent then we bring everyone together and we all work on the project. And we also have external staff members in our network, who help us cope with the volume of work."

The combination of an awareness of tradition and high-speed, the flowing transitions between atmosphere, fictions and intelligent convertibility characterise both the office space and the work method of the Edge Design Institute.

"I really want to create a totally informal environment in the office." When Chang comes into the office he goes up to the DJ console and makes music. This place of intensive work is also a cinema, bar, and living room with a sofa designed by Chang on which colleagues can spend the night when working long shifts. A hammock came back from the contribution to the Venice Biennale 2002, a large red ping-pong table is used for brainstorming, client presentations, taking meals together, but also sometimes for a game of ping-pong." I have a lot of personal stuff in the office," Chang says. "All my colleagues have a lot of personal things here also, maybe they feel at home in the office, too."

OVER THE ENTRANCE ONE CAN READ THE EDGE-CREDO ON A LED SCREEN:

"The EDGE of certain things depends upon one's own perspective. An EDGE can be a fuzzy shadow or a boundary line containing a definite blue print. An EDGE is not as rigid as implied; alternatively it may be fluid."

The Edge Design Institute is located in a former warehouse, the five-metre-high space is divided into two levels, the lower one is separated into four areas: "the multifunctional hall, the timber house, the garden and the metal box. Each is the scale of about four metres, like the traditional tenement home with 3.6 metres. I am very traditional."

On the lower level of the metal box are the workplaces for the staff with a view of the harbour. Chang has his own area on the upper level. "Here are my objects, my toys. This space is more private. Actually it is also my home. It is a library, a club, a copying centre. Each area is transformable. This warehouse has been my favourite building for a long time. When I stand up in front of the window, I won't be able to see the land on the opposite side of the harbour, you see only water and cruise boats. You feel like you are on top of a very high cruise boat."

Chang's own city, Hong Kong, which finds itself in a permanent state of transformation, is an inexhaustible source of inspiration. "I have a big collection of Hong Kong guides. Dense, hybrid intensified, this is Hong Kong, but it is global. There is a lot of research on tight space, on small space. But in our case we are in the real situation all the time. We are always in the battlefield with the tight situation, and we are so fast here. It is time condensed into instant time." Spatial economy at all scales is also a source of inspiration. Chang collects small and tiny objects with unusual qualities.

GARY CHANG SENT THIS SKETCH FOR HIS NEW OFFICE TO HIS STAFF FROM ABROAD. →

"Actually it is also my home. It is a library, a club, a copying center. Each area is transformable."

WestoverHau 13062004

"Treasure boxes, compact boxes, storage boxes, simply small objects, these are key areas of reference." Cardboard models are built on the long table with the pieces of Lego on it that stands in the "garden zone" where walls and floor are clad with green carpeting. Small boxes that close in clever ways or are ingeniously subdivided are studied intensively, repeatedly taken up for closer examination. The sources of inspiration are dealt with in a clearly focused way. During a lunch taken together the screen becomes a cinema. For Chang film is the ultimate interplay of creative inspiration and condensed time. "A lot of times I am most clear in the cinema. Movies have the power to make you high, it lets you connect all the key issues you are thinking of, you find the references much more quickly." Using a pen with a built-in light Chang sketches or makes notes in the darkness of the cinema.

However different the strategies of inspiration may be, the time factor is always eminent. "People are checking from one media to the other, half or even more than half of their life is checking. I don't know how productive you can be or creative." Chang compares checking the news to tidying up. "My key agenda is how to do creative tidying up, physically and digitally. If you have a nice system it helps your design process a lot." As he is talking about cleaning up he looks across at his desk with its stacks of books; before the piles of books topple over he tidies them up, uses this activity to rediscover them.

GARY CHANG'S SKETCHES FOR GARY'S APARTMENT

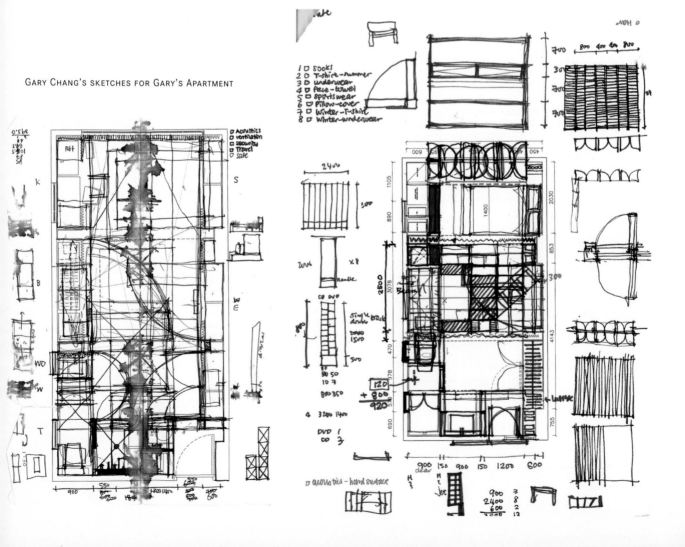

"I see connections. I am so interested in finding similarities. I find the tidying up process quite creative sometimes, it requires a lot of technique, it is clearing up your mind. Don't you think it is so nice if you clean a place and at the same time it is a design process?"

For Chang handling the creation process efficiently forms part of the theme of sustainability and comes under the heading "smart use of resources. When you start to work, time really flies. We have to be very selective in what we do, it is about sustainability in life." Chang builds oases of slowing down into the acceleration machine that is his working life: "When I fly to Europe, I don't go to the airport just two hours earlier, but five to six hours. In the airport lounge I have my private cabana. This is a total privilege. I calm down and enjoy. I play hide and seek at the airport, like a detective story, I control my privacy, my area of concentration."

GARY CHANG

"Movies have the power to make you high."

GARY CHANG

"Actually the view is not the urban area but also the natural environment. You feel like you are on a boat. You look down and you see only water."

I am a craftsman

Yona Friedman

STUDIO APARTMENT
33, BOULEVARD GARIBALDI
PARIS
FRANCE

FIELD RESEARCH IN THE STUDIO APARTMENT IN SEPTEMBER 2007
AND FEBRUARY 2008, PHOTOGRAPHY, DISCUSSIONS WITH
YONA FRIEDMAN & TEXT: ELKE KRASNY

"Architecture is not a paper game. A model does not give you reality. It is a reference. Even the photomontage I like to use is relative to the real. I did my first photomontage in 1959. My colleagues laughed at me, but it is of course not a joke. It contains information, even though it is not precise information people know it immediately. I did my photomontage on Paris because it was impossible to explain it verbally." Since the 1950s the architect and thinker Yona Friedman has developed his concepts of "mobile architecture," "the realisable utopia" or the "ville spatiale" that, while visionary, are also close to the social circumstances that shape our reality.

Since closing his studio more than ten years ago, his apartment in the same building has served as a centre point of inspiration, production and of his life. Everything, be it the walls, floors or ceilings, are covered with collected or self-made pieces, not a single centimetre is left unused. The corners are occupied by veritable towers of packing material such as cardboard, or WC paper rolls. He uses this industrial waste and the simplest of materials such as wire and paper as the initial materials to provide a structure for his models and collages.

Since 1957, when Friedman — who was born in Budapest and studied in both the Hungarian capital and Haifa — moved to Paris, no. 33 Boulevard Garibaldi has been the place where he receives visitors and researchers for discussions and to exchange ideas. His apartment embodies the concept of the "ville spatiale" which is based on the largest possible space for expression and the maximum freedom of the individual within a given structure.

"My desk is like a shelf. I know where everything is. I move here or there with my hands. It is not a desk, it is a shelf. There are cut photographs, there are keys, there are all my materials. On my table I know where to look for it."

For his "Manuals," which he produced with UNESCO in large numbers in the 1980s, he developed a comic-like language of image and text that is inspired by the cartoons he made in the 1960s.

"I draw very fast. To draw slowly takes away all the pleasure." To sketch or draw Friedman sits on a basket-chair beside his desk with a thin black fine liner in his hand and balances a squared or unlined writing block on his knees. "I am an A4 man. When you draw, the line is different on a large sheet of paper, the hand movement is just not the same on a large sheet. The quality of the line is very important. It is about the connection between the hand and the eye. You know, it is a combined operation. You imagine and at the same time it corrects itself as you draw," says Friedman.

YONA FRIEDMAN

"Innovation is always conservative."

Yona Friedman is connected to the world by a fax machine. He took his leave of the computer decades ago, although in its early days he even developed his own design programme. "The computer programme I did in the 70s, it was too worked out, too abstract, too fast for people. The computer gives you the best decision for the computer, but not the best decision for real people." He sees his photomontages and models as providing guidelines for other people, views his handcraft approach as creative potential and seeks to escape from the limitations of preconceived computer programmes.

"I decomputerized in 1973. There is a lot of dictatorship in the computer. All the pre-fabricated software has implications that are not stated. I am not free to use them as I want. It would be better to simply teach people how to do their own software. Computers give no real choices. With paper, it is different. I can crumple it, I could not do this by computer."

For the models the A4 format generally also provides the starting point. "The other thing I often work with is models, series of models. Not just the small ones, but also the real size." In the last few years Friedman has worked together in realising mobile architectures with museums, cultural facilities or universities. "I generally ask people for the photographs.

YONA FRIEDMAN

„The computer gives you the best decision for the computer, but not the best decision for real people."

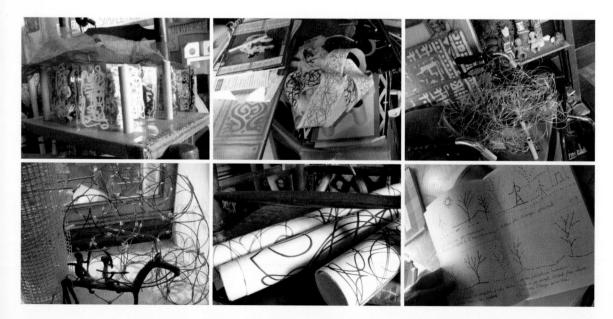

Very often there are places I know, like now with the Architekturzentrum." Then he draws over the photographs and sends them back by post or fax. "I draw directly on the photograph. It is near to reality, no, it gives you an idea of reality. It is a sketch for a non-professional."

At present he is building models for a bridge between Shanghai and Pudong and has a vision for a graffiti museum that would be made available for collective inscription, and a street art museum that can be run by local cultural initiatives in public space.

"They look at how I am making the model and it is ready to be implemented locally. This is very important for me because I do not travel so much any more." In the workshops his formulas are used according to individual ideas. "In mobile architecture you have trial and error. You don't know it on paper. You know it only in real scale. Even architects don't know it, only reality will show. This is why I am so much involved with real scale. All the things I proposed I at least tried out once at real scale. I know how they look, how they taste, how they feel. I know that they can be done." "Mainstream architecture" as Friedman sees it is characterised by "over-planning." "I think really for me architecture is very, very different from mainstream architecture. Things are more than architecture. My method is closer to the

YONA FRIEDMAN
"My desk is like a shelf."

YONA FRIEDMAN
"Drawing and text together are a universal language."

medieval craftsman. There was no over-planning but merely a following of instructions. I am trying to allow architecture to create itself. All my drawings represent a possible stage in a long process. Building means a long process." What is ready-made constantly requires intervention, Friedman says. Space in which action can be taken is created by means of mixing, transformation and the use of imagination. "Mixing is the most primitive, popular level. It is open for everybody. Transformation is one level higher. But to imagine it is the highest level. Imagining what the outcome might be. What I estimate highest is to imagine it."

Whereas for a long time Friedman was interested in the possibilities of industrialisation as a way of increasing the degree of individual freedom, today he is fascinated by the relationship between post-industrialisation and improvisation. "Your first step is this and your second step is that. Things are differently made in every place. Do it as you like! This is a completely different attitude to a normal architect's way. It is a public improvisation."

"Do it as you like!"

22/01 '08 10:22 FAX +43 1 5223117   ARCHITEKTURZENTRUM WIEN   001/001

Graffiti museum
in the courtyard of AzW

Nature as a tool

Antoni Gaudí 1852—1926

1898—1914 STUDIO ON THE CONSTRUCTION
SITE OF THE COLÒNIA GÜELL
SANTA COLOMA DE CERVELLÓ, ÀREA
METROPOLITANA DE BARCELONA, SPAIN

FIELD RESEARCH IN BARCELONA IN MARCH 2008
CONVERSATIONS WITH JUAN BASSEGODA NONELL,
LAIA VINAIXA, JORDI FAULÍ I OLLER, MARTA HERNÀNDEZ I ROIG,
FERNANDO MARZÁ PÉREZ, SÍLVIA VILARROYA & TEXT: ROBERT TEMEL

Unlike most of his contemporary colleagues Gaudí did not come from a line of architects, his father was a coppersmith. Gaudí questioned classic methods and historical model forms and used nature with its wide variety of curved, structurally optimised forms as his most important source of inspiration. However, unlike the approach favoured in Art Nouveau, he did not use nature just as a source of ornament but also found in it models for the forms of his spaces and structures. He attempted to translate the models he discovered in nature into building materials, a process in which abstraction played an important role. As a graduate of the young architecture faculty in Barcelona Gaudí was trained in a number of technical subjects and therefore could understand the physical, logical and geometrical laws of natural phenomena. And hence the crypt of the Colònia Güell near Barcelona is the first building in the history of architecture to employ a hyperbolic paraboloid, a form that occurs in nature and for which formwork can be relatively easily built. Using the standard design tools available at the time, which were for the most part plan drawings, it was impossible to develop something of this kind. Gaudí was distrustful of drawing, even though he had financed his studies by working as a technical draughtsman. Despite his talent in this area he drew as little as possible, attempting instead to work out the form of the building by means of collaboration with the skilled workers on the building site and through the use of models. In the case of large, complex projects such as the church for the Colònia Güell, and the Sagrada Família church collaboration on site was not enough and Gaudí had to develop new methods: firstly the hanging model developed for the Colònia Güell, which is without parallel in terms of its dimensions and complexity, and later in Sagrada Família plaster models of various sizes up to a scale of 1:10 which served as examples for the stone masons and bricklayers. Gaudí also examined building forms by means of graphical structural studies.

Gaudí received the commission for the Colònia Güell from his long-standing patron, the industrialist Eusebi Güell. The Colònia is an industrial complex outside Barcelona with workers' housing based on English models of philanthropic capitalism, built by Catalonian modernist architects. Gaudí was commissioned to design a church there, which gradually increased in size during the years he worked on the design with the result that after Güell's death his heirs withdrew the commission – which explains why only the crypt was ever built.

Next to the building site Gaudí erected a site hut, something he also did in other important projects such as the Casa Milà and the Sagrada Família. In 1898, in this hut, work was started on the construction of a hanging model that was continuously improved over a

LEFT PAGE: GAUDÍ'S STUDIO IN A HUT
ON THE CONSTRUCTION SITE, COLÒNIA GÜELL.

MALE MODEL FOR THE DECORATIVE
ELEMENTS ON THE FACADE, SAGRADA FAMÍLIA.

period of ten years. Gaudí travelled three times each week from Barcelona, where he had his studio at the Sagrada Família building site, to Colònia Güell, where he worked with two or three of his staff from the afternoon until the evening. In addition he also dealt closely with about a dozen workers on the building site directly beside the hut.

The suspended model was based on the principle of the catenary. If the line taken by a flexible hanging chain is inverted it describes an upward-pointing arch; in stone arches that follow this line only compressive forces occur, no tensile forces, which is to say the arch is structurally optimal. This also means that the arch cannot rest on vertical pillars, the pillars are inclined to follow the line of the catenary and lead continuously into the arch. The principle of the catenary perfectly reflected Gaudí's conviction that the functionally optimal form is also the best one aesthetically. Gaudí's preference for natural form corresponds with a deep Catholicism that accounted for his limitless, almost monk-like dedication to monumental building commissions from the Church.

The chord model at a scale of 1:10 with a total height of four metres and a length of six metres hung from the ceiling of the site hut in the Colònia Güell. A scale of 1:10,000 was chosen for the weights, so that the model weighed around 400 kilos. Gaudí used chords to determine the geometrical shape of the pillars, arches, walls, vaults, domes and towers of the

ORIGINAL PHOTOGRAPH OF GAUDÍ'S HANGING MODEL

PHOTO: ILEK INSTITUT FÜR LEICHTBAU ENTWERFEN UND KONSTRUIEREN, UNIVERSITÄT STUTTGART

planned building, and little pouches filled with lead pellets to simulate the forces that arise. On the chords that represented columns, pieces of woods showing the cross-section of the column were fixed. In the hanging model each part was dependent on the whole and every change led to a change in the inclination and direction of the other strings and therefore of the building elements. By changing the chords and weights the model arrived at the structurally optimal form by itself, so to speak — it was in a certain sense the precursor of modern-day parametric design methods. The spatial system of the hanging model allowed forms to be created that could not possibly have been arrived at using the methods of calculating or drawing available at the time.

The sculptor Vilarrubias photographed the hanging model. For the photos pieces of cloth were inserted at places in the model to represent the areas of solid wall. Gaudí used these

ANTONI GAUDÍ PAINTED OVER THE PHOTOGRAPHS OF THE SUSPENDED MODEL.

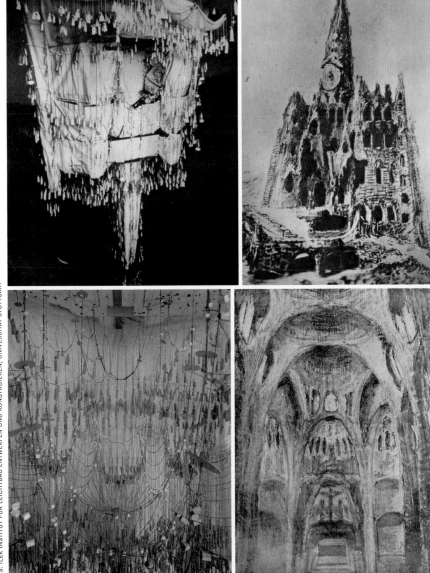

Gaudi used these photographs. He turned them upside down and painted over them.

photographs, turning them upside down to paint over them so that he could examine the form of the building both inside and outside. Then, using the chords, the dimension, position and direction of every building element could be worked out and constructed on the neighbouring building site. The model was also used in making detailed drawings for a number of elements. After completion of the hanging model in 1908 construction work on the crypt was carried out for a number of years.

Gaudí's presence was regularly required to translate the complicated model into the structure of the building. When he fell ill for a number of months construction work had to be suspended for the duration of his illness. In 1917 the project finally came to a standstill.

REFERENCES
Burry, Mark (Hg.) (2007) Gaudí Unseen. Die Vollendung der Sagrada Família, Berlin.
Martinell, César (1975)Gaudí. His Life, his Theories, his Work, Barcelona.
Tomlow, Jos (1989) Das Modell. Antoni Gaudis Hängemodell und seine Rekonstruktion:
neue Erkenntnisse zum Entwurf für die Kirche der Colonia Güell, Stuttgart.

CONSTRUCTION SITE, COLÒNIA GÜELL

ORIGINAL PLAN WITH MARKS FOR THE MODEL TO BE HUNG UP.

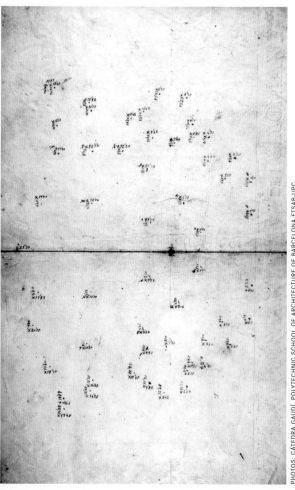

THE CHORD MODEL WITH PIECES OF CLOTH IN GAUDI'S STUDIO HUT.

PHOTO: ILEK INSTITUT FÜR LEICHTBAU ENTWERFEN UND KONSTRUIEREN, UNIVERSITÄT STUTTGART

The suspended model was based
on the principle of the catenary.

Designing in bed

Lux Guyer 1894–1955

1944–1954 OFFICE IN
ZURICH
SWITZERLAND

FIELD RESEARCH IN SÄFA AND ITSCHNACH AND
RESEARCH AT THE GTA ARCHIV/ETH ZURICH IN JUNE 2007,
CONVERSATIONS WITH BEATE SCHNITTER UND DOROTHEE HUBER
& TEXT: GUDRUN HAUSEGGER

"The small triangle is a typical 'Luxli instrument'. She used it when designing, generally lying down on the bed or on a couch. Reclining like Madame Recamier was something of a habit in our family. I can see her now in front of me drawing, supporting herself on one side and sketching with pencil or pen in a tracing paper block. Then she sometimes took this small triangle. I never saw a scale to go with it," Swiss architect Beate Schnitter recalls her aunt Lux Guyer who opened her own office in 1924 as one of Switzerland's first female architects.

Swiss art historian Dorothee Huber has described Lux Guyer's work as an "architecture of the centre," meaning by this term an approach that showed an unconstrained openness to the innovations of the avant-garde but also demonstrated a levelheaded bourgeois side. "As an architect of her time she remains individual in stylistic terms, making it difficult to place her in any particular group," Huber explains in greater detail. Despite, or indeed perhaps because of, this position Guyer was successful and had numerous different kinds of commissions and well-known clients. One of her particular concerns was to respond to the housing requirements of the modern woman and to create quality living space, as she demonstrated in her residential buildings for single women, students or elderly people. She drew simple coloured floor plans for the future tenants of her buildings to give them a better understanding of the relationships between the various spaces.

During her most successful period in the 1920s and early 1930s Guyer had up to 25 staff in her office in Zurich's Bahnhofstrasse. It was largely women who chose to work in her practice. "But Lux Guyer was not born to collaborate, she didn't hand over responsibility and did not accept designs from others. All that she left up to her employees was the production of the detail drawings. In her innermost self she was completely certain of things," says Beate Schnitter. She sought collaboration with colleagues from the field of applied arts, whom she regularly called upon to help with the decoration and fitting out of public buildings.

Lux Guyer did not follow the traditional path of training as an architect but acquired her knowledge in a variety of ways: in courses at the Kunstgewerbeschule (school of applied arts) and at the ETH in Zurich, on her extensive travels, or as an autodidact in England. "In London she went to the reading room in the British Museum every day," Schnitter emphasises. This kind of training was probably responsible for Lux Guyer's very simple, almost childish drawing style. "She only worked in offices briefly, for short episodes, never long enough to acquire her own style or to adopt the style of a master," Dorothee Huber adds. Her working drawings are strikingly colourful in comparison to the generally restrained use of colour in the

LEFT PAGE: LUX GUYER AND HER "HOMEMAKER' SCHOOL"
BELOW: MUSEÉ IMAGINAIRE, LUX GUYERS' SOURCES OF INSPIRATION

Lux Guyer collected newspaper clippings and pasted them on to index cards. She kept these sources of inspiration in a wooden drawer.

1920s. Lines and areas are often emphasised with pink or light blue, the edges bordered with golden paper. This tendency towards colourfulness in the design phase closely reflects the particular context of her work: the study of colour, its various shades and the way they interact with the qualities of light and reflections in a building was an area that Guyer made very much her own. "Lux Guyer herself talked in this respect of a mix of light. In the SAFFA Haus she used a total of 17 colours. Hers was an artistic colourfulness, not a graphical one. She used white only from 1937 onwards," Beate Schnitter explains.

In a small wooden drawer with an alphabetical index Guyer archived objets trouvés and her sources of inspiration: excerpts from newspapers, illustrations of furniture, postcards, and notes. This private collection is what is known as the Museé Imaginaire that Guyer used when designing. Schnitter recalls: "She read a great deal. And it was above all at night that she read — and designed."

One of her particular concerns was to respond to the housing requirements of the modern woman.

LUX GUYER AND HER STUDENTS IN THE ARCHITECT'S GARDEN

PHOTO: GTA ARCHIV / ETH ZÜRICH

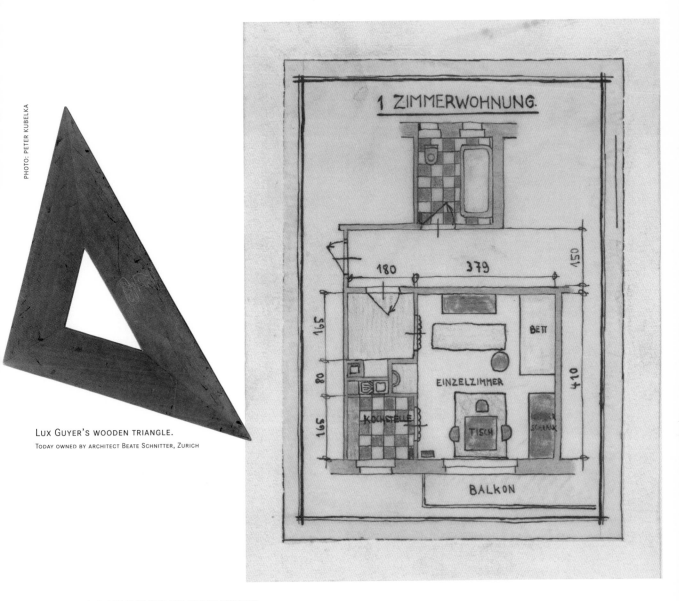

1 ZIMMERWOHNUNG.

180   379   450

165   80   165   410

BETT

EINZELZIMMER

KOCHSTELLE   TISCH   SCHRANK

BALKON

PHOTO: PETER KUBELKA

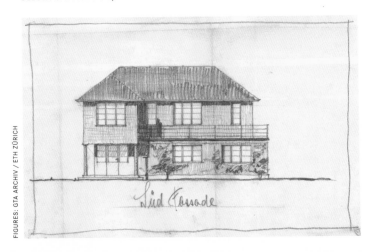

LUX GUYER'S WOODEN TRIANGLE.
Today owned by architect Beate Schnitter, Zurich

RIGHT ABOVE: FLOOR PLAN FOR THE FUTURE TENANTS
OF THE WOMEN'S HOUSING PROJECT LETTENHOF
BELOW: SAFFA HAUS, COLOURED DRAWING SOUTH FACADE

Süd Fassade

FIGURES: GTA ARCHIV / ETH ZÜRICH

The small triangle is a typical Luxli instrument.

She drew simple coloured floor plans for the future tenants of her buildings.

It starts on 5×7

Steven Holl Architects

450 West 31st Street
New York
USA

Field research in the studio in January and August 2007
Photography, Conversations with Steven Holl, Chris McVoy,
Partner und Rodolfo Dias, associate and staff members
& Text Gudrun Hausegger

The first impression you gain upon entering the office of Steven Holl Architects on the 11th floor in midtown Manhattan is one of concentrated activity but without any sense of hectic rush. Whereas Steven Holl once regarded number of players on a football team as the ideal size for his studio, he now explains that, with the increasing number of commissions, this concept has changed. A total of 35 staff members of different international origins now work in the loft-like open plan office. All the work stages, from model building to detail drawings, are carried out here. The shelving system in which architectural magazines and books are stored defines the layout of the workstations, while at the same time offering a display area for innumerable models.

Steven Holl's own office, which adjoins the large open plan space, has a direct view of the Hudson River. Occasionally this architect, who grew up in Washington State on the west coast of the USA and therefore has a close relationship to harbours and the sea, takes up his binoculars to read the names of the ships passing by. The shelves are full of books and grey boxes in which he keeps his chronologically ordered sketchbooks. A number of his watercolour drawings hang casually on the walls and several models are displayed here, too.

"The process starts always on 5 x 7 inches. Sometimes it is just a painting, it is not necessarily a built one. Might be a building later, might be a piece of furniture," says Steven Holl, describing his design process that is typified by clear, regularly repeated procedures. Holl uses watercolours to commit his first ideas about a project on paper in sketchbooks measuring 5 x 7 inches. He draws everywhere, in his office, in his weekend house on the Hudson River and during his travels, when he uses a smaller travelling set of watercolours. These small but often highly detailed drawings are the starting point for every design and provide the conceptual basis for the architect in the office that is responsible for the particular project. The drawing that shows Holl's fundamental design idea is scanned and then further processed digitally. "With the advent of the computer the little watercolour became supercharged, because I can scan it and I can send it. The process became much more efficient," Holl explains the standardised design process. For every project there are a number of watercolour drawings and, depending upon the duration of the process extending from the crystallisation of the idea to the construction of the building, they are generally distributed in several sketchbooks. "Steven's watercolours are kind of a conceptual guide for us, to guide us through the development of the project," explains Chris McVoy, Steven Holl's partner in the New York office.

STEVEN HOLL

"With the advent of the computer the little watercolour became supercharged."

All the other steps are examined in the course of numerous discussions between Steven Holl and the project architect, at times also with the entire project team in what are called pin-ups. Now and then solutions are developed over a lunch with the entire office. Often people from outside, who are close to Steven Holl professionally, are invited to offer their critical opinion. Holl incorporates the results of these discussions or pin-ups in new water-colour drawings that are then integrated in the production process of the particular project.

Each of these work stages is accompanied by innumerable models built at different scales and from very different kinds of materials. It is not unusual for up to one hundred models, consisting of competition, design, working and presentation models, to be made for a project. Many models are made using traditional "hand craft" but where a certain precision in the presentation or high speed in the production is required new technologies such as laser cutters or 3D printers are used for the production. Many of the models are hybrids of old and new technology. "It is always about sculpting the space, engineering the space of the project. Even Steven's watercolors have that sense already in them," says Chris McVoy.

Steven Holl also works regularly together with his wife, Brazilian artist Solange Fabião. This cooperation can range from critical reviews to close collaboration, in terms of both concept and implementation, over the entire duration of a project.

"I believe that architecture in the 21st century could come from any inspiration. In the 19th century the idea was that architecture must come from architecture and it has a

"This is my office messy, messy like an artist studio. I kind of like the mess. I see something in the mess that becomes part of my creativity."

precedent whether it's a typological precedent or a precedent in Greco-Roman language. I think in the 20th century we had the functionalism and the relation of expressivist structure. Once we reach the 21st century there is a freedom and I believe that the source and the connective link could be a piece of music, could be a scientific principle, could be a relation to a morphology that is in the ground of a particular place. So the source of the inspiration is an open question and something unpredictable. I think that is a positive opening for architecture." In principle for Holl the place where a building is to be made and the relationship that the building should have to this place provide the definitive inspiration for the design. "So rather than having a style that I repeat on all these different sites, I try to have a new architecture for each site and situation, trying not to have a personal style," explains Holl.

Despite having buildings on site in the USA, Europe and Asia Steven Holl spends a lot of time in his New York office. Much of the necessary communication is dealt with using new technical facilities such as video conferencing, Skype or web cams that allow building sites to be "visited." But despite all these new channels of communication certain presentations still have to be made in person. And so every five months Holl flies to Beijing where, since the end of 2006, he has run a second office and is carrying out a multi-functional building with the support of a project architect and a staff of twelve. However, the global expansion of Steven Holl Architects has not changed this office's typical design process. "It is a process that I use to this day, all the time," confirms Steven Holl.

SKETCHBOOK AND 3D-STUDIES SOLANGE FABIÃO: CITÉ DU SURF ET DE L'OCÉAN IN BIARRITZ

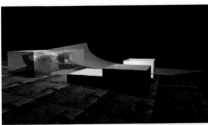

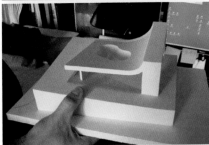

SOLANGE FABIÃO
"I am originally from Rio de Janeiro and surf has been part of my live as well as of Steven's."

STEVEN HOLL
"The concept drawing I did in collaboration with my wife Solange Fabião."

Six million miles

The Jerde Partnership

913 Ocean Front Walk
Venice
California, USA

Field research, photography, interviews with Stuart Berriman, partner, design principal and Tom Jaggers, partner, chief technical officer and conversations with numerous members of staff & text: Elke Krasny

"Last year Jerde staff members travelled a total of six million miles. Travelling is part of the design methodology. It is crucial to get to know the feeling, the atmospheric side of the site," says Wendy Arrington, one of the 100 staff members who work for Jerde Partnership at Ocean Front Walk in Venice Beach. For this globally engaged architecture firm the design process often begins in the airplane, flying to the location of a new commission. The coloured markers are packed, and a couple of rolls of tracing paper are also included in the luggage. Jerde Partnership's speciality, "place making," starts with the search for the typical, the analysis of the authentic that provides the initial material that is subsequently transformed. "The design is very much tailored to the place," explains Stuart Berriman, one of the head designers. "We work all over the globe. We get as close as possible to the DNA of the place, to the genetics of the place."

In intensive workshops the design principals and directors of design develop the basic characteristics of a project with local clients. "We'd go to the site for a day but we'd be in the town for a week. We'd have a series of workshops throughout the design process that would bring us back to the place. The going back is important, you develop ideas with the colleagues here in Los Angeles and then you test them, to see if they fit or not."

Research souvenirs from all around the world, such as the sand samples filled into little Granini bottles, demonstrate the strategy of integrating in the design process in a material way locally discovered information that is specific to the particular place, and using it as a quotation of authenticity. "We collect things on site to tell the story we try to embrace. That's the fun part." "We keep all the designers here in Los Angeles because of the collaborative approach," explains Wendy Arrington describing the firm's strategy of co-creativity. "After the first meeting, after they come back, they distill this creative process. They let it ferment and grow." Research forms the basis for the development of the design on a number of levels: market research, location analysis by means of local strategies, specific local forms, colours, materials, scale, light or forms are researched in books and Internet, printed, copied, hung side by side on the walls. "Coming up with the big idea is the most collective activity, almost a purely creative process. You are looking through a childlike eye. We let ideas flow as many and as far out as possible. Ideas can come from a junior designer or Jon himself." "Draw a movement, draw a line, very early on," is how Wendy Arrington describes the work process of "their visionary," Jon Jerde and emphasises what highly unusual tools, including even lipstick or paper for wrapping bread in, are used for this first line. "Senior designers come up, he

STUART BERRIMAN

*"At the beginning
we all meet in
Jon's room."*

offers his insight. They almost think the same," she says. "Jon Jerde gets involved, a lot of my colleagues get involved. We collaborate with the clients very well. They always feel it is their design as much as ours." Sketching plays a central role in the group work situation. "We'll sketch. The sketching process is often lost in the computer age, but it becomes so critical when you are designing in a group. When you have the confidence to draw things out in front of the clients you can get their involvement immediately."

The individual work areas where the staff draw are on the upper floor. The reception, meeting rooms, their own copy shop and a model building workshop are at ground floor level. Often many people work together in a team In Jon Jerde's dark room — that doesn't face towards the ocean — and has a huge casino gaming table. Pencils lie ready for use in the hollows originally intended for the jetons. Thanks to the internal network plans relevant to the particular discussion can be shown on the flatscreen at any time. Sketches are busily made during all discussions and meetings. "Very early on in the process we all get together in the big room and we'll present to the specialist consultants on water, graphics, landscape, lighting what we know about the project. In the same way that we blur between our work and their work they will not be fighting over whether that element is a light element or a landscape element or a water element. Since we make places more than buildings we would involve these people very early on. If you walk through the office you will see that everything is very integrated."

STUART BERRIMAN

"The DNA of the place, the genetics of the place ..."

Tracing paper is always at hand during discussions with technical consultants and structural engineers. "With the sketching it goes right through till the end of the process. With 30 people solving a problem, our role as architects is to mediate. You quickly get out a piece of paper, stick it on the table and you start drawing on it, you can lead it your way and not their way. That is probably the strongest tool we have as designers: the ability to lead the process by drawing in the right direction." A ventilator revolves unceasingly in the group work room on the side of the building facing towards the ocean. It is too windy to open a window, the sketching paper and the photocopies would be blown away. The results of the research work, the respective city plan and most recent printouts of the stage the project has arrived at are fixed to screen walls with drawing pins.

"Experiential design" attempts to grasp the various atmospheres and specific characteristics of a place. What a place narrates are the experiences that it allows. An essential element in "place making" is the planning of temporal sequences as a dramaturgy of experiences. Streets or paths are discussed in terms of their potential for allowing experiences, or as structures of time. "It's not a themed process." The "underlying structures of how the streets work, how people work with spaces" is evoked by images. The coloured print-outs that show local characteristics hang beside each other, indeed sometimes over each other, so as to develop solutions to problems by means of visual clusters of themes. The groups are given key

Jon Jerde's sketches for Namba Park in Osaka 1996

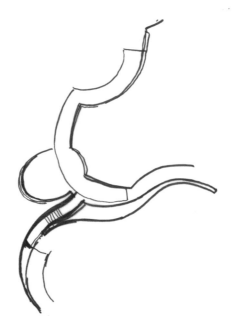

Jon Jerde

"Draw a movement, draw a line, very early on."

words, the organising terms are written between the images using a black fineliner. The relevant city plan is always hung on the wall. "It is about using local materials but in an appropriate contemporary way." Inspiration and possible activities are visualised just as much as urban planning considerations and architectural features. "Sketching and research at the same time," is how they describe this process. Communication with the clients is not just by means of plans or models but also through images and texts.

"A developer's mind is always oriented towards comparing his or her formula to other projects in the world. What the client looks to us for is: 'is it going to work', and we have to ask ourselves who is it for." The considerable amount of discussion and collaboration involved takes some getting used to. "It is quite a learning process" for newcomers to the firm. "This can take between six to eighteen months." The key to collaboration as a design method and to "integrated design" as a process is the management of the staff resources. The firm has its own human resources department. Janis Jerde, Jon Jerde's wife, directs the "staffing meeting" held every Monday. During lunch hour, a time for which the client cannot be charged, all the project managers responsible discuss the distribution of work in the individual projects. "Senior designers stick with one design process. All the senior people are knowledgeable of all the projects," says Wendy Arrington.

The staff can bring their own tools according to their needs and their likings.

The changeover to computer took place in 1988 and 1989. "There is no possible way to produce the buildings we have produced in the last 15 years without computers. Computers inform the process of design. Of course computers have changed very much the way we work on a timeline. The whole electronic transfer is so quick, the Building Information Modeling we are starting to use now compresses timelines."

The collaborative process, which is repeatedly emphasised, is also found at the level of technologies. "The computer is a tool to reinforce what we do naturally. The collaborative process between 3D, 2D, model making and sketching happens within a design team," which for Stuart Berriman represents one of the major differences to the way other architecture firms work. The initial concept development phase takes about one month, and is then followed by a phase of assessment and reworking. "The schematic phase lasts about three or four months," the entire process including detailing takes, on average, nine months. "The speed is actually something that helps to create a process. We are quite good about bringing together smart people and you get far more in a fast process than in a slow methodical approach."

JON JERDE'S SKETCHES FOR NAMBA PARK IN OSAKA 1996

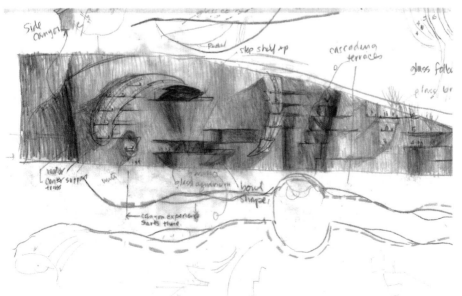

STUART BERRIMAN

"That is probably the strongest tool we have as designers, the ability to lead the process by drawing in the right direction."

Suspicion towards tools

Lacaton & Vassal

206 RUE LA FAYETTE
PARIS
FRANCE

FIELD RESEARCH IN THE STUDIO IN APRIL 2007 AND FEBRUARY 2008
PHOTOGRAPHY, DISCUSSIONS WITH ANNE LACATON,
JEAN-PHILIPPE VASSAL AND STAFF MEMBERS & TEXT: ELKE KRASNY

"It isn't the line that expresses the idea; it's not the line your hand draws that gives you the idea. It's precisely the other way around. If you know something exactly then you draw it," explains Anne Lacaton. The many possible lines that could be sketched distract the gaze from the right, essential line. "You draw a line and aren't very sure about it. Among the hundreds of lines there probably is not a single one that is the right one," stresses Jean-Philippe Vassal. In the design process the central thing is the maximum freedom of the imagination. The power of imagination is restricted by sketching, by every method of making something material; the phase in which options are left open while thinking things out is terminated far too quickly. "The things you think cannot be equated with writing, with drawing, with making models. As long as you have them in your head and only there, they are free, they can be easily changed." Their method of working is not confined to a single workplace or a method. The process never stops. "Even when you are not in the office and you still haven't found the solution together, you continue thinking. You write something down or call up your partner. But you always have the project in your head, even when perhaps it only continues to work in the back of your mind," adds Anne Lacaton. "Nothing is really fixed," Vassal points out. "A project develops for the most part through discussions, but also through plans in the computer." They reject fixed routines. "There isn't any fixed place to start off from, sometimes it is here, sometimes on the building site, sometimes somewhere else." Nonetheless, there are specific moments that characterise the way they work. They work out a great deal with words, through discussions with others. There are far more colourful plastic chairs in the studio than there are members of staff. You can always pull up a chair, sit down beside someone at his or her desk, look at something in the computer and discuss it. Lunch is generally eaten together, meals are picked up from a nearby Chinese restaurant, fruit is sliced up and the coffee machine is on the go the whole time. "It's really important to spend more time in the office alongside people you enjoy being with," says Vassal describing the work atmosphere, which is calmly concentrated but seems to have no inner feeling of pressure or tension. "We have here a good place for talking and thinking, a good mood." Despite how important talking to each other is, they take an ambivalent and critical stance to the acknowledged ambiguity of speech. "At the moment I prefer writing to discussing. When you talk there are so many misunderstandings," Vassal says, questioning language as a design tool. "At the end a great deal is lost," emphasises Lacaton. The problem lies in translation. For me, in my imagination things are very, very clear, but when I explain them then they aren't so clear any more," says Vassal.

ANNE LACATON

"We do not want to leave traces."

"You collect decisions. In the end all the decisions fit together and that makes the project."

Thinking out architecture is described as freedom of imagination. The precision that results from reduction hones the potential of the possibilities. Jean-Philippe Vassal uses an analogy to describe how the individual parts ultimately and consistently all come together. "When I do a crossword puzzle then I just think of the empty grid, and when I'm completely certain in all directions I write all the answers in at one go, because if you write in a single answer and it is wrong then you will never solve the puzzle. I like to leave things in my imagination." It is the parts, which ultimately fit together, not the preconceived idea of a whole thing produced by these parts. "A project is created through a sequence of decisions. You collect decisions. At the end you see that all the decisions fit together and this constitutes the project," explains Anne Lacaton. Jean-Philippe Vassal recalls the architect Jacques Hondelatte, for whom he and Anne Lacaton worked after their studies in Bordeaux. For Hondelatte there were two ideal states of architecture. "A project is at its best when you dream of it or when it is finished, finally built." The process in-between has vanished. In the office of Anne Lacaton and Jean-Philippe Vassal there is little that indicates the traces left by the work process. "We don't want to leave traces," Anne Lacaton says. "We look at as many things as possible," Jean-Philippe Vassal adds. "A project never starts with absolutely nothing, it always begins with a specific situation," Lacaton explains. What already exists is important for making a start. So that the possible development of a project can remain indefinite for as long as possible and to avoid overhasty decisions, they delay producing illustrations. "In fact the important thing is the question of doubt, the possibility of remaining open to change".

ECOLE D'ARCHITECTURE DE NANTES, PROJECT DESCRIPTION

1. INTRODUCTION

PROCESSUS DE PROJET

L'origine du projet se fonde sur le sentiment qu'habiter un bâtiment, éloigné de sa raison première, produit une situation magique, étonnante, différente.
Les bâtiments se réduisent souvent à vouloir coller au plus prés d'un programme.
Le projet que nous proposons se situe en amont du calage du programme.

1. Création d'un site

Nous proposons une **construction primaire** qui constitue une prise de position et un seuil dans le processus de projet.

Elle s'implante sur l'îlot principal au maximum du gabarit autorisé et comprend :
- une structure en béton armé : poteaux, poutres, planchers
- 3 planchers d'une portance de 1000 kg/m2 et superposés à 9, 16 et 22 mètres (toiture) et d'une surface totale de 10 450 m2
- une surface au sol de 4 510 m2
- une rampe extérieure accessible aux véhicules
- 2 noyaux de circulation verticale

La construction primaire est basée sur des grandes portées dans un principe économique, permettant aussi une grande liberté de l'aménagement intérieur et d'évolutivité.

La capacité portante des 3 planchers permet l'installation de structures secondaires et d'éléments préfabriqués portant par répartition sur ces planchers.

Sa compacité et ses hauteurs divisibles en planchers intermédiaires crée une capacité importante de surface appropriable, permise par l'économie et la configuration du projet.

2. Installation dans le site

La construction primaire est le site de départ pour l'installation du programme de l'école d'architecture.

Nous proposons à ce moment du processus de projet, d'engager un travail avec l'utilisateur de l'école d'architecture pour définir l'installation dans la construction primaire.

Un catalogue d'outils, de matériaux, de systèmes permettant d'occuper la structure et de s'y installer est élaboré. Ils mettent en œuvre les conditions techniques, climatiques et de confort nécessaires pour rendre habitable la structure primaire.

Les outils sont de technicités et de coûts parfaitement adaptés aux caractéristiques particulières des différents types d'espaces. Ils répondent aux normes de construction, de résistance au feu et d'acoustique. Ils permettent de construire les espaces traditionnels du programme dans les parties d'espace brut de la structure, de façon confortable, légère et remaniable.

Le catalogue comprend :
- les planchers intermédiaires
- les structures secondaires
- les façades

Les planchers intermédiaires divisent les volumes entre planchers principaux en hauteurs compatibles avec les activités du programme.
Les structures secondaires (ossature métallique ou bois) délimitent les enveloppes des entités programmatiques.

Les façades créent deux types de climat dans la construction primaire. Le bardage polycarbonate crée un climat protégé, bio-climatique, abrité du vent et légèrement chauffé. Les baies vitrées coulissantes, ouvrent sur des coursives, crée un climat chauffé (normes programme).

L' économie du projet se définit en fonction de deux type d'espaces.
- les espaces résultants de la construction primaire, extérieurs, intérieurs protégés
- les espaces aménagés correspondant au programme

La volonté affirmée de réaliser l'opération strictement dans le budget a conduit à mener parallèlement les choix de projet et la vérification économique simultanée. Cette démarche intègre la notion d'économie dans la phase de conception pour maîtriser les choix et leur faisabilité dans leurs pleines cohérences.

La méthode classique de coût au m2 quelque soit la surface, ne nous semble pas satisfaisante dans le cas de ce projet, car elle ne permet pas de tenir compte de la hiérarchie et des caractéristiques des différents espaces.

3. Proposition d'installation du programme

Dans ce processus, le projet remis dans la phase concours constitue une proposition de réalisation du programme de l'école d'architecture dans la construction primaire et une exploration des capacités de cette structure.
Elle ouvre la réflexion, qui peut être reprise en amont, au seuil de la structure primaire, dans un dialogue concerté avec l'utilisateur.

Le plan d'urbanisme et les espaces publics qu'il crée, nous amène à choisir la densité pour l'implantation de l'école d'architecture. En plus de la construction sur l'îlot principal, le projet propose de construire aussi sur l'îlot côté Loire au maximum du gabarit autorisé : bâtiment structure métallique, façades vitrées.

Dans le bâtiment principal, le parking est réalisé en superstructure dans le volume du niveau 0 (0b et 0c). Cette option représente une économie importante. Le parking est conçu comme de la surface utile potentielle au cœur du bâtiment, construite au coût du parking et convertible à tout moment.

Le niveau 3 est une esplanade extérieure sur le toit. Elle peut recevoir des activités de l'école (construction), des évènements extérieurs temporaires, concerts, cirque, des terrains de sport.

Au total le projet propose une surface hors œuvre brute de 26 500m2.

The issue is precisely reducing what is potentially possible, extracting the essential. "I've never written poetry but I imagine you probably erase about the same amount of things as you write," says Jean Philippe Vassal. "We try to not to think in an a priori way and we also try to listen as precisely, sensitively and respectfully as possible."

If the client wants to see something then drawings have to be made. "It becomes necessary to draw because the client wants to see drawings. And then we can draw it immediately, in two or three hours. And we are entirely amazed by this fact. We think that the drawing will take two weeks but in fact everything is ready within two hours and this line, the early line of the project, will also turn out to be final." The work processes are neither strictly formalised nor organised in a rigidly hierarchical way. In the office people treat each other in a considerate and friendly way. "It is not just the two of us together, it's often not very well organised. Often it's very informal. At times it might be more efficient to be very strictly organised but we don't work that way."

They have their studio in a former tailor's in a commercial building. "We were lucky, before this we were in the Palais de Tokyo. Here we have exactly the kind of situation we like to work in. It is quiet and bright," explains Anne Lacaton. "The space is remarkably generous. You can move around, you can work here or there." Lacaton and Vassal sit together with their staff, ten architects, a graphic designer, various interns at different times, and a secretary in an open plan studio. Both the load-bearing structure and the traces of the previous use of the space are clearly visible as is the technical infrastructure; the cables hang from the ceiling,

ECOLE D'ARCHITECTURE DE NANTES

JEAN-PHILLIPE VASSAL

"A project is at its best in your dream and also when it is finished, totally built."

producing their own choreography of usefulness above the desks. A piece of African material hanging on one of the columns encloses a large leg of ham. When they take an aperitif together or after a period of intensive work Anne Lacaton carves some ham for everyone.

This light-flooded space is remarkably bare, but with poetic moments. Material of the kind used in glasshouses provides protection against too much sunlight. Members of staff often walk along the wide corridor, sometimes listening to their mobile phone, as they withdraw to a more sheltered area at the back that is separated by a sheet of glass.

This is also where Jean-Philippe Vassal grows his orchids. "I have had orchids for five years. They are mysterious. They're not hybrids, they come from Chile, Ecuador, Columbia and from specific regions in these countries. We are in Paris. And I have a globe nearby and I look at where they come from." The orchids need attention, care and are a powerful inspiration. "A little world," Anne Lacaton says. "It's interesting to dream about places, too," says Jean-Philippe Vassal.

"It is not a tool and is all tools," Vassal says. The office has had computers since 1985. "We take the ones that are efficient. But we don't want to make ourselves prisoners of a tool. Tools, which they do, indeed like, should be simple. "Like the BIC ballpoint pen. I like it because it's a beautiful object." "Cheap and simple," adds Anne Lacaton. "It's really astonishing the way the ballpoints circulate through the office. I'm certain I use a different one every day." For Anne Lacaton the problem with the computer lies in its excessively fast precision, decisions that are made too quickly. "With the computer you arrive at a precise solution very quickly, a precise rendering that gives you an idea at a very early stage. One of the things that this tool means which while not dangerous is somewhat problematic is that you make decisions too fast." The sole potential that Jean-Philippe Vassal sees in the computer is as an archive of comparisons. Although they don't use this method in the studio he does

JEAN-PHILIPPE VASSAL

"You can not do architecture with physical tools."

employ it when teaching. "We don't do this in the office, but with our students. Everything exists already. Moods, atmospheres, contexts. You could probably recombine and re-organise architecture by transforming and redefining fragments taken from different places. This means that architecture can be real images, real moods that one effectively combines in a new way and adapts to local situations. Making a lot of photographs is an interesting tool, I think and then working with them. We don't photograph all that much. But what is interesting about the computer is that you have a large number of photographs in it and can reorganise and classify them, make assemblages with them." The goal is more reality, not more virtuality, a greater amount of collected empirical material that can be combined in different ways by the computer. "It's got absolutely nothing to do with virtual forms and volumes, but with more real evidence that you can combine in new ways." The issue is never generating form, finding a single, decisive form. "It's never about form. It is always a collection of fragments," says Anne Lacaton and talks about "micro-moods. Not in order to define the situation with an image but to produce ten or five or twenty micro moods, a new mood."

Had Jean-Philippe Vassal to opt for just one tool, then he would do without all of them. Architects can never stay at the scale of reality with their tools. And this is where they see a great difference to filmmakers and also to users of architecture, who move within a real scale. "I think that a film-maker doesn't work this way, he's always within the scale. How can you make a building like a shirt that you put on? Or how can you be architect and resident at one and the same time. That's really difficult," says Vassal.

"Tools can be a little dangerous. I am suspicious of tools," says Jean-Philippe Vassal. Freedom lies in reducing the number of tools, not in making oneself dependent on their physical characteristics. "An architect's most important tool is his mind. Of course, the other tools are important but they can change. You can't make architecture with the concrete tools."

JEAN-PHILIPPE VASSAL

"For five years now I have had the orchids. They are mysterious."

"The most important tool for an architect is his head."

Sketching with millimetre precision

Rudolf Olgiati 1910–1995

1938–1940 OFFICE IN ZURICH
1944–1995 OFFICE IN FLIMS-VILLAGE,
SWITZERLAND

FIELD RESEARCH IN FLIMS-WALDHAUS AND FLIMS-DORF AND
RESEARCH GTA ARCHIV/ETH ZURICH IN JUNE 2007, CONVERSATIONS
WITH ALFRED CANDRIAN, MARIANNE FISCHBACHER, PETER MÄRKLI
AND URSULA RIEDERER & TEXT: GUDRUN HAUSEGGER

"With all the passionate enthusiasm at his disposal Rudolf Olgiati transformed a knowledge derived from classic modernism into something completely new. Combining this with a further formative 'experience' that he found in houses in the Engadine valley led in a series of stages to his buildings' individual expressiveness," explains Swiss architect Peter Märkli, discussing his older colleague's work. And so amidst the Swiss mountain world of Graubünden an architecture developed that embodied a deep understanding of local building traditions and a broad study of both Greek building methods and of Le Corbusier. "He was convinced by the cubist considerations of Greek architecture that he got to know through his intensive study of Le Corbusier. He rediscovered this in the architecture of Graubünden, but also in old furniture from the Romanesque and Gothic periods. Until the middle of the 16th century this furniture was marked by a cubist way of thinking. His investigations in this area sparked his interest in detail. When the feeling for old building traditions began to disappear in the 1960s Olgiati could not understand why. He began to collect all these objects," says architect Alfred Candrian, who worked with Olgiati for years.

The collection that developed in this way is a comprehensive one: from solid wooden doors to carved chests as well as smaller and tiny pieces such as pottery vessels, cutlery and shards. Every single piece was systematically archived and entered in an inventory with a number and details of where it was found. Olgiati collected with the idea of returning some of the pieces to where they had originally come from. "He included many of the pieces in his buildings in a fragmentary way, as a kind of aesthetic sensation, a contrast, and as a link to old building traditions," says Candrian. He used above all old double doors that had to be left untreated so that the wood could become "bone hard," as Olgiati put it.

He also derived important inspiration for his buildings from the items he collected. From them he developed an understanding of many elements of construction, for example the way in which chests or table legs are stabilised by tectonically perfect struts. And this kind of constructive pragmatism was also reflected in his design process. Like in classic Greek architecture, Olgiati saw the column as an important constituent element that had to be employed correctly. "Olgiati used the mass of a column to define a place. But he gave it a 'shadow' at the top instead of a capital, as it is not structural in nature," Peter Märkli explains Olgiati's use of hollow columns with cut outs at the top edge.

He kept the collected objects in a barn beside his house in the village of Flims. He converted the Graubünden farmhouse, transforming the dwelling into an office: the former

FIGURE: GTA ARCHIV / ETH ZÜRICH; PHOTO: HANS-PETER SIFFERT

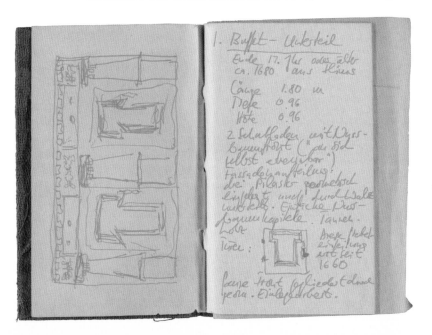

LEFT PAGE: RUDOLF OLGIATI AT HIS DESK IN HIS STUDIO, THE FORMER PARLOUR
RIGHT PAGE: RUDOLF OLGIATI'S SKETCHBOOK WITH NOTES ON ONE OF HIS FOUND OBJECTS

ALFRED CANDRIAN

"Rudolf Olgiati's most important tool he always had on him was a B6 pencil."

main parlour became the main office space, the other parlour a second smaller study in which
the helio-copying machine was kept and the library was housed. Three re-occurring themes
among the books there reveal Olgiati's interests: books about and by Le Corbusier, about local
building traditions, and cookery books. He generally worked with three or four people, mostly
students. "It was like working in a family, there was never anyone who did just one kind of
work," Alfred Candrian recalls.

For Rudolf Olgiati the starting point of each project was always the particular situation
of the building site. The first ideas, generally very concrete impressions that he brought with
him from the site, were pursued in the office in intensive discussions with his staff. "This all
took place in a very unconventional way in the kitchen while drinking coffee and eating small
pastries that he always picked up from the baker himself. Or we thought about things at the
open fire," Candrian says. The first sketches were made in a block of thin tracing paper sheets
that lay ready for use on a table directly beside the fireplace. Olgiati regularly withdrew, made
his ideas more concrete, and returned to discuss them again with the others and to make
further drawings. "These were sketches into which everything flowed, from the most
fundamental considerations to Greek architecture, to Graubünden architecture, down to
colours and textiles," says Candrian. Often a second sheet of tracing paper was laid over the

RUDOLF OLGIATI

"You do not have to travel in order to understand."

SKETCHES ON TRACING PAPER, APARTMENTHAUS LAS CAGLIAS 1959–1960

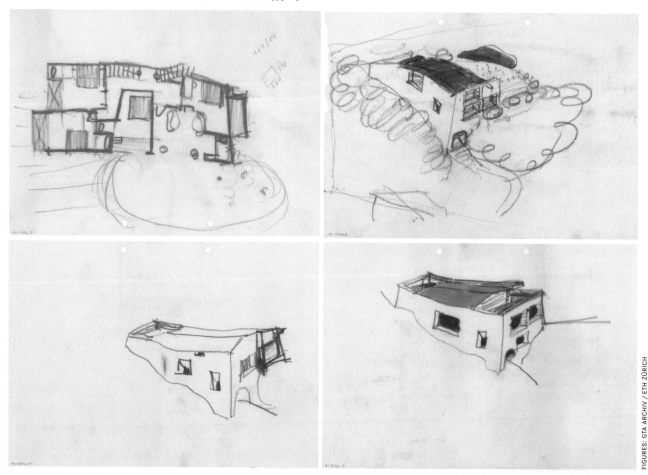

first one, but generally everything was concentrated on a single sheet. "Whatever remained valid at the end was then reworked using strong lines drawn with a soft B6 pencil. Or sometimes he took colours such as indigo, vermilion and green. This made the unimportant things fade into the background," Candrian recalls. Olgiati was not only economical in his buildings; he drew on the top half of the sheet of paper and then folded the lower half over it. This explains why there are numerous sheets on which the sketches are mirror-symmetrical. The B6 pencil was Olgiati's most important design tool and he always carried one with him. His sketches were detailed and extremely clear in terms of proportions and dimensions. "You could measure from these sketches almost down to the millimetre. His certainty about proportions and scale at the sketching stage was astonishing," says Candrian. In some cases these designs could even be used as technical drawings, in other cases they formed the basis for such drawings made by his staff using the standard tools of the time such as the T-square and the setsquare. The plans for building permit applications were drawn in ink on tracing paper and reproduced using the helio copying machine. For Olgiati the process did not stop during construction; he regularly came to the site with new sketches and intervened to make corrections. "Sometimes he drew parts he regarded as particularly important on wrapping paper at a scale of 1:1 and brought them with him to the construction site. One of these elements was the arch, which he said should not be straight at any point. When he was dissatisfied with parts that had already been built, he had them taken down," says Ursula Riederer, who was able to gain a deep insight into Olgiati's work in the course of a book and film project about the architect. He seldom made models. He had a good three-dimensional sense himself. He convinced his clients with sketches and explanations. The possibilities offered by the computer as a new kind of tool fascinated him. But he was not prepared to integrate this innovation in his office. For him the sketch remained the most important medium.

SKETCH ON PAPER, APARTMENTHAUS LAS CAGLIAS 1959–1960

WOODEN DRAWER, ONE OF THE TRADITIONAL OBJECTS RUDOLF OLGIATI COLLECTED

PETER MÄRKLI

"Were I to show architecture in the style of Le Corbusier to someone, then I would choose the lobby in Las Caglias."

Enthusiasm for the void

Charlotte Perriand 1903—1999

1956—1999 Studio
15 rue Las Cases
Paris
France

Field research in the former studio of Charlotte Perriand
in April 2007 and in February 2008, photography and
interview with Pernette Perriand Barsac & text: Elke Krasny

"It all came to her so easily." Charlotte Perriand's daughter, Pernette Perriand Barsac, who worked in her mother's practice for 25 years, cannot recall her using specific rituals to start work. Charlotte Perriand created a sheltered and concentrated place that she could withdraw to behind a woven timber screen in her studio. But Perriand did not confine her sketching and designing to her workplace, a former garage that she converted herself, but also worked during meetings, or in restaurants. She drew very rapidly, using different instruments, in ink, with hard oil pastels, sometimes also at a very large scale on parcel paper or cardboard, preferrably with hard H7 pencils.

"I don't create at my drawing board (...) The drawing is only to fix, to control the idea. I create in the factory, at the craftsman's, in front of the machine, with the material and after I have questioned the engineer or craftsman in detail about the qualities of the material or the methods of fabrication." (PERRIAND 1942) For ten years, from 1927 to 1937, Charlotte Perriand worked as a designer in Le Corbusier's studio in the corridor of a former Jesuit monastery in Rue de Sèvres. Although the Corbusier chaise longue became famous through the iconic photograph of Charlotte Perriand reclining on it, in fact behind all the pieces of tubular steel furniture now regarded as classics, the chairs, chaises longues, beds, cupboards, were the result of collaboration between three persons: Le Corbusier, Pierre Jeanneret and Charlotte Perriand. Perriand kept a 140-page sketch book, the "Livre de Bord," during this period, and today we can approach her development process through the facsimile documents in the volume of the same name published by Arthur Rüegg.

Perriand's drawings are proof of both her analytical research that focussed on the needs of the human body, and of her close collaboration with craftsmen and producers: "What she always draws (...) are the equivalent of the fullsize shop drawings done by her artisans with all the holes, bolts, screws, and rods that make her furnishings function smoothly. The large scale drawings are executed with elegance and grace and provide much more information than the usual bare minimum." (SCHREIBER AUJUME 1998: 244) But drawing was not the only important means of design and reflection: models, photography, photo-montages also played an important role for her. Perriand also used photo-montages to express her social concerns and political convictions, like in the wall piece "La Grande Misère de Paris," which she showed in 1936 at the Salon des arts ménagers. In using aesthetics as a weapon in the class struggle Perriand combined her closeness to both nature and technology as well as her passion for the avant-garde and for local handcraft traditions, whether it was in in Japan or in the French

PHOTO: PERNETTE PERRIAND BARSAC

CHARLOTTE PERRIAND

"I create in the factory, at the craftman's, in front of the machine, with the material."

Alps, where she built her own chalet with coursed walls of local stone and, together with Guy Rey Millet, designed "Arc 1600" from 1969 onwards and later "Arc 1800" with Gaston Regairaz as a mega-resort, a city in the mountains for democratic mass winter tourism.

Even today the studio of Perriand (who died in 1999) reveals her attention to detail, as affectionate as it was precise, her examination of the economy of space which she developed with the utmost consistency, her rational organisation, her practical and functional considerations, and her attentive use of materials. It seems as if each of the things there stands in the place that was intended for it and which it could then occupy. The creation of order, the avoidance of superfluity and clutter, the concentration on what was necessary and tangible, and the attempt, even in the tiniest space, to create a feeling of emptiness and lack of clutter relate to Perriand's exact study of everyday activities and procedures as a prerequisite for design. What she needed for her work, her collection of patterns and samples of materials, her pencils, the ink, the oil pastels, the paints — all vanish behind sliding elements, into cupboards and drawers. In 1940 Perriand went to Japan, after that country entered the war she moved to Vietnam, where she acquired and deepened her knowledge of weaving, wood, rattan and other natural products, only returning to Europe in 1946. Her passion for Japan — from summer 1954 she once again spent a year there — is atmospherically present in the studio, in the design of space as well as in the tools: bamboo ladders, arrangements of plants with stones or Japanese oil pastels. In the research she carried out in Japan Perriand did not rely solely on her gift of observation but attempted to grasp the laws and structures of the materials and the organisation of space by taking measurements. (CF. ZENNO 2003: 91)

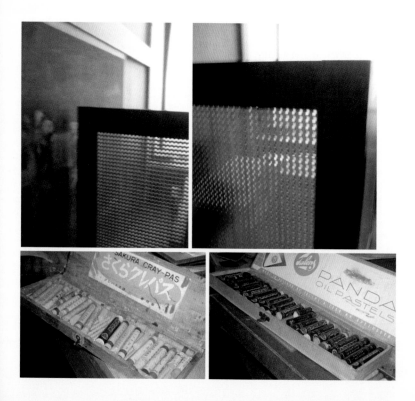

Autochthonous, traditional techne could delight her just as much as the latest technological possibilities and developments in materials. Her daughter Pernette Perriand Barsac recalls that her mother was fascinated, for example, by surf boards, and she adds that if Charlotte, who was also a passionate skier, had been twenty years younger she would certainly have taken up surfing. The mountains and the sea were the places from where Charlotte Perriand drew the energy she needed for her work. Pernette Perriand Barsac remembers her mother saying: "I really must empty myself to charge my batteries."

REFERENCES

Barsac, Jacques (2005) Charlotte Perriand Un art d'habiter 1903–1959. Paris: Éditions Norma.

CharlottePerriand (2005) Éditions du Centre Pompidou, Paris.

Modelling Charlotte Perriand (2006) *A Project by Sadie Murdoch,* Henry Moore Institute Leeds

Perriand, Charlotte (1942) Contribution à l'équipment intérieur de l'habitation au Japon. Tokyo: Editions Kugio Koyama, zit. nach: *Barsac, Jacques* (2005) Charlotte Perriand. Un art d'habiter. Paris: Éditions Norma.

Rüegg, Arthur (Hg.) (2004) Charlotte Perriand, Livre de Bord 1928–1933, Basel: Birkhäuser.

Schreiber Aujame, Edith (1998) Working with Charlotte. Pp. 244–245 in McLeod, Mary (Ed) (2003) Charlotte Perriand. An Art of Living. New York: Harry N. Abrams.

Zenno, Yasushi (2003) Fortuitious Encounters. Charlotte Perriand in Japan, 1940–41. Pp. 90–113 in *McLeod, Mary* (ed) (2003) Charlotte Perriand. An Art of Living. New York: Harry N. Abrams.

RESEARCH FOR THE DESIGN OF THE MAISON DE THÉ, UNESCO PARIS, 1993

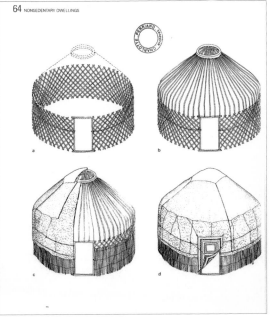

CHARLOTTE PERRIAND

"I must empty myself to charge my batteries."

SKETCHES, MAISON DE THÉ, UNESCO PARIS, 1993

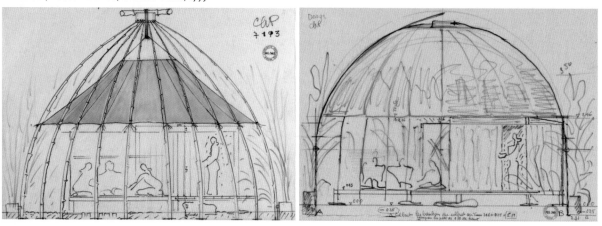

PLAN, MAISON DE THÉ, UNESCO PARIS, 1993

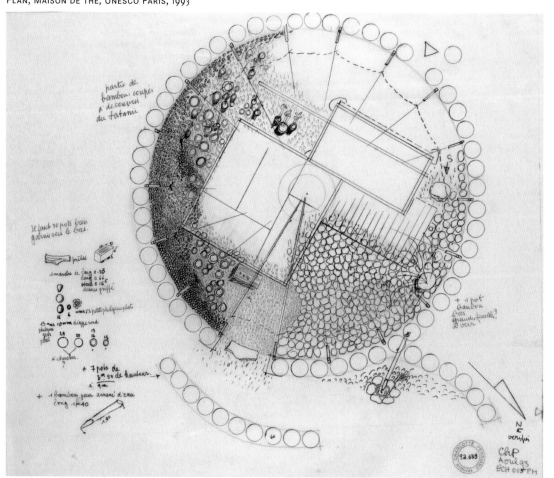

CONSTRUCTIVE DETAIL, MAISON DE THÉ, UNESCO PARIS, 1993

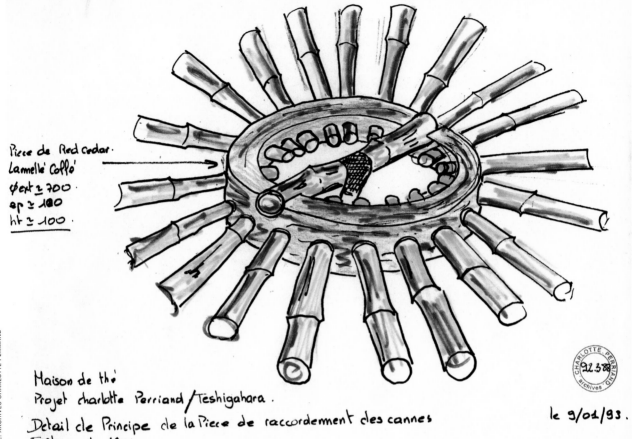

Piece de Red cedar.
Lamellé Coffé'
ϕext $\simeq$ 700.
ep $\simeq$ 100
ht $\simeq$ 100.

Maison de thé
Projet charlotte Perriand / Teshigahara.
Detail de Principe de la Piece de raccordement des cannes
Faitage du dôme.

le 9/01/93.

PERNETTE PERRIAND BARSAC

"She drew very rapidly."

Deleuze on masochism, a tool for architects

R&Sie(n)

24 Rue des Maronites
Paris
France

Field research in the studio in February 2008
cameraman Giuseppe de Vecchi, interview with
François Roche & text: Elke Krasny

"I am a pure schizophrenic in the Deleuzian sense," says François Roche, almost before the door has closed behind him. Although the studio opens onto the street front with a large display window, it offers no indication that it is a place where architecture is produced. Ambiguity elevated to the status of a methodology characterises the practice of R & Sie(n). Bubblewrap, the transparent and yet opaque plastic material used to line crates when transporting artworks, covers most of the studio walls like a kind of curtain. There is no right to a view inside. R & Sie stands in neon letters on the window pane of the shop front, which Roche compares with Duchamp's "Large Glass". For more than two years the studio has been based in these premises in the twentieth arrondissement of Paris — an area with a high proportion of immigrants and artists — which was previously used by Chinese as a tailor's. To Roche the immediate surroundings of the studio seem "hard, like in Berlin".

"So of course it is a pure schizophrenic sensation, that something is new. But in fact we avoid seeing how much we are slaves of the sensation of newness. We are trying to do our best to develop the sensation of uniqueness and to write a scenario, a protocol that could engage a possibility of uniqueness, while including the recognition of the illusion of the process." Action is always preceded by knowledge about something already in existence, about the informed handling of an endless supply of references. The beginning is fed from a long story of what came before and applies this existing knowledge as a process of reflection with quotations ranging from Kafka to Leibniz, from Schwarzenegger to Deleuze, or from Foucault to Artaud. "This is a 'No Entry' interview," Roche declares, sitting down on one of the grey Fatboys in the front area of the studio behind the glass pane and looking outside at the "no entry" traffic sign on the far side of the street. "So it's a game where I try to avoid to reveal any part of my work or process, no entry, restricted area. It is a kind of toxicity if you go inside. There is a kind of risk. What the design is carrying is a story, a part of the danger. It is interesting to start with a restricted area."

Each beginning differs in the conscious use of the illusion of uniqueness. "It is a postmodern way of producing, always linked to a kind of mimesis, of copyism, you rewrite a concept, because you consumed something before. You are reintroducing something from your educational background." The way in which every new project begins therefore does not follow an established ritual, nor a recipe that has achieved the status of certainty through repetition. "It would be labyrinthine to articulate the line of a project. The starting point of each project is the notion of situationism, where we could extract from a situation the

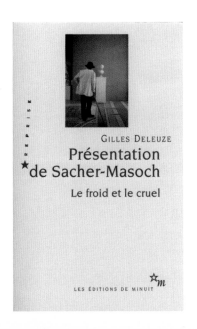

GILLES DELEUZE
Présentation
*de Sacher-Masoch

Le froid et le cruel

LES ÉDITIONS DE MINUIT

FRANÇOIS ROCHE

"It is a tool for architects. The servitude could be reversed, the victim could be the dominator."

ambiguity of its own transformation." From the existing, what is already there, the possibility of what could be there, the potential of becoming is shaped by the strategy of an interpretative re-reading. What is at stake is to think about the elements that are decisive for the possibility of transformation, "the ingredients which could carry the transformation and at once promote the development of the situation and resist its own development." Leibniz' Monad appears as a model, not in terms of its universality, but as a concentrate, as a compressed extract of the specific. In this sense the issue is "the here-and-now-position, the recognition of where we are." As a result of reflecting on the here and now for the start of one of their latest projects the office bought a gun. The "Cold War" and the demilitarised zone between North and South Korea, which has been recaptured by nature and is now a wilderness undisturbed by humankind with a diversity of animal species, resurfaces in the design act as a mimetic production using a gun and clay blocks. Somewhere between "Mephisto effect" and "Faust effect" it is the gun that plays with the "idea of danger". "We bought the maximum gun you can buy in France, the minimum you can buy in the US, the maximum you can buy here, I prefer to be here, minimizing the gun addiction. We bought this kind of weapon to understand the ballistics through a clay box. The bullet holes corrupt, deform and twist the substance and create a shape."

Shooting "could create firstly a geometry, secondly, simultaneously, the porosity of the volume." The model, the clay block perforated by the shots, which was subjected to violence, is then completely destroyed in order to understand the geometry of the holes made by the shots. To grasp its innermost quality it is taken apart, sliced into elements that inspire and

FRANÇOIS ROCHE

"The tooling re-prodcues the unique attitude."

R&SIE(N) PROJECT „HE SHOT ME DOWN" 2006–07, HEYRI/KOREA. SITUATION: SOUTH KOREA JUST IN FRONT OF THE NORTH PART, TOUCHING THE DMZ AND JSA (DEMILITARIZED ZONE AND JOINT SECURITY AREA ZONE). ROBOTIC DESIGN WITH STEPHAN HENRICH. CREATIVE TEAM: FRANÇOIS ROCHE, STEPHANIE LAVAUX, JEAN NAVARRO. WITH MARION GAUGUET, LEOPOLD LAMBERT, ANDREA KONING, IGOR LACROIX, DANIEL FERNANDEZ FLORES.

guide the parametric design process. The next step in the design consists of cutting up the clay block into pieces. "The most interesting effect in this ballistic production is the morphology, topology production, is the impact of the sound. We could re-read and reinterpret the morphology through scanning. We try to understand how the 3D could be combined with parametric designs, to understand the 3D, to analyse and reinterpret the geometry, through a process of constructions, of analysis and realisation, without losing the randomness system. We cross this logic of production by standardisation. We cross the bridge from irregularity production of nature to a reasonable reshaping through a logic of assembling, where we immediately lose this random, irregularity topology of nature, but we try to keep the bad way in the process." The story is always hidden deep in the story unfolding its potential for the imagination of the users only through the holes and cracks. "The story is like an apparatus to articulate relationships. The story is not a story for itself, in its own value, it is a clue, a key to articulate relationships. When you reread fairytales, it is incredible how they include blur parts. There is always this misunderstanding or misreading in a perfectly linear process of writing, a kind of disconnection or disruption of narration where your imagination, your subjectivity is immediately going to inflitrate the narration, to feed the narration with your own stories, because of the gap in the narration. Stories for us is not telling stories in the tradition of the novel as a pure description of something. It is vague, a vector which could help us to include blur, misunderstanding." The disruption in the linearity of stories can take on many forms. The masscultural associations seep through the cracks and folds of the stories. The point where the bullet emerges from the clay block reminds Roche of a flower, the flower

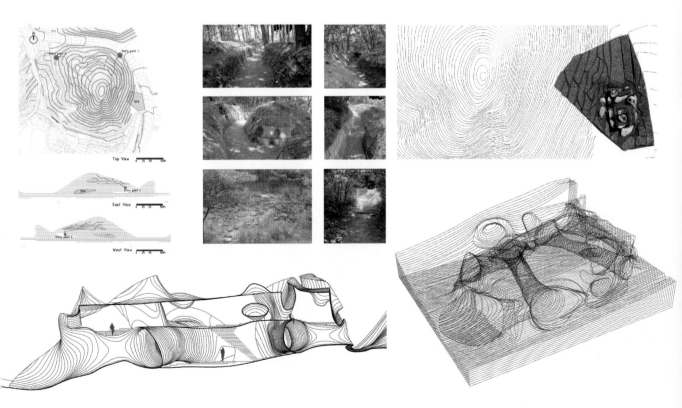

FRANÇOIS ROCHE

„We never do the same thing twice."

in Terminator 2, where the liquid Terminator transforms into just such a flower. All the references are constantly invoked in the course of speaking. "That is for the bad mass media culture, a subculture reference, but it is of course part of the world, we have to accept these subcultures as a fragment of our reality."

Roche believes that the possibilities offered by computer technologies contain the potential to reverse the relationship between object and aura, within the logic of mass production. "If we could reverse the Walter Benjamin notion of the lost aura, we rediscover it through computing, through processings, through computer protocol, through digital design, through parametric design; we rediscover the ability to produce uniqueness. We are able to rediscover through mass production, with the tooling of the mass production the uniqueness of the architectural answer to a specific site." The tools play their decisive role in the game of the production of architecture. In contrast the completed project is merely a "fragment of the story". The issue is not the proof offered by building, by the ability to build, the emphasis is on what points beyond building, the network of stories, the narratives that are spun and can be spun further by means of the respective project. "We have the tooling now but no longer the story. Before it was the other way around, the story was still intact, but we did not have the tooling to participate in it. Now architects are confronted by the tools we are using to make the appearance of something rare, but we do not know why."

The most important tool for architects is, he says, the essay that Gilles Deleuze wrote about Leopold Sacher-Masoch's Venus in Furs. "By means of this protocol, the servitude could be reversed, the victim could become the dominator. This is a very interesting tool of now, how the monstrosity has to be protocolized, in a way by this kind of contractalization, it could be modified, it is a tool for architects."

FRANÇOIS ROCHE

"Like an old robotic witch coming from the forest."

In the office people work in a very concentrated way, it is very quiet, but all the same there is a lot of talking, music is often played. Stephanie Lavaux generally functions as the DJ. They listen to "word music, not world music". "Foucault, Deleuze, the recorded voice of Bachelard." For the design process for the project in Korea all of them listened to Antonin Artaud's 1947 radio programme Pour en finir avec le jugement de Dieu, which was forbidden in France for many years. And Artaud is also involved in the answer to the question about hand sketching in the office. "It is clear that Artaud is saying we shit, we write. It is just an extension, where the tooling is incredibly open, even the very archaic one, of course. Sometimes from the archaic one we chose a pure speculative, fictional one. Real tooling to code and to recode the complexity." Roche emphasises that they never do the same thing twice but here too the self-reflectivity of what is asserted is elevated to a spiralling game in which what has just been maintained is immediately questioned. "It is an enormous pretension to declare this never-twice attitude." In the use of tools the issue is the calculated play with what cannot be calculated, opening up to allow the unpredictable as an element of design, rescuing the productivity of chance and what is not predetermined. Consequently Bernard Rudofsky's Architecture without Architects acquires a different dimensionality in terms of questioning the architect's position of omniscient authorship.

"We are really dreaming of an architecture without architects where the architect does not claim his own superiority, his own authorship to justify his genius by integrating all the components. We love to lose control, we love to integrate the possibilty of losing control, we fail to kidnap it all in one frame or to ensure our authority. We try to never dominate our subject, it is of course a lot of work, we try to be dominated by our subject, it is a reversing of the process, we are weak or a slave, in servitude to the story itself."

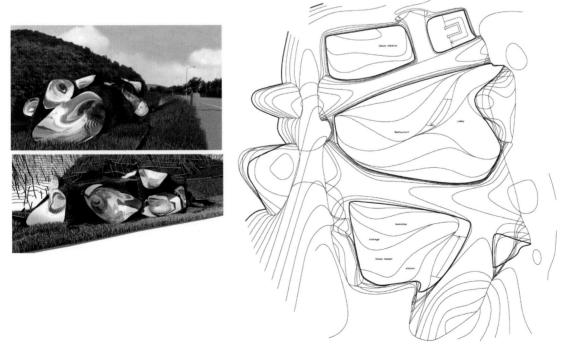

Françios Roche

"We are a non-macho agency."

The machine: Hopefully,
it happens in the mind

Theiss & Jaksch / Schwalm-Theiss & Bresich

SCHWALM-THEISS & BRESICH
ALTGASSE 21
VIENNA
AUSTRIA

FIELD RESEARCH IN THE ARCHITECT'S OFFICE IN SEPTEMBER 2007
AND IN JUNE 2008, PHOTOGRAPHY, CONVERSATIONS WITH GEORG
SCHWALM-THEISS & TEXT: ELKE KRASNY

"The sketch is a way of moving things ahead, of getting the solution onto paper, but I don't actually sketch all that much," says Georg Schwalm-Theiss. Pencils are good for making sketches, but he doesn't have a favourite brand or degree of hardness. Small pencils, sharpened many times, that were received as promotional gifts — "the one from Bene is really good" — and white A4 sheets are used for sketches, but also white trace. The sketch is not celebrated in any way. "It isn't kept or stored." As early as 1984, at a time when computer workstations were still very expensive, Georg Schwalm-Theiss already saw that the future of making architecture lay with the computer and invested in "the machine," as he likes to call this tool. "You can't fudge anything with a computer." Because he doesn't work with the computer himself he needs printouts to develop projects and to think them out further. "I need the simultaneous, I find the sequential way things are presented on the monitor difficult, I have to have the things lying in front of me." I draw something up, pencil something in roughly" but, even more than sketching on paper or drawing on computer printouts, it is the discussions with staff that advance the design process. They seldom build physical models. The 3-D simulations are a "genuine alternative to the model". The design process always starts with an intensive examination of the site. "Of course it is the site. I mean, it really says something." And they don't just visit the site once, but repeatedly, they study and analyse it. The inspiration that develops as a result of looking at and understanding the topography are decisive for the design process. "Very often it is what the site and the terrain offers, what comes from the plot. This is a source of joy. Designing for the steppes is far more difficult. Schwalm-Theiss takes snapshots while inspecting the site. The issue here is "the act of photographing that reminds you of things later". It is the action that counts for noticing and remembering. The act of documenting is far more important than what is documented. Decisive is not what can be seen on the photographs but the fact that they were taken. The act of recording something by photography evokes memories far better than the snapshots produced, which often are not even looked at again during the work process.

"If something doesn't occur to me immediately then I do something else. It continues working internally someway or other; hopefully this happens in my head. When you've nothing to do you think about a particular job quite a lot. When you' don't have much to do, you reflect a little. These are all chains of thought that are continued. I make notes on scraps of paper. When I go jogging I have time. Probably you should always have a notepad with you, but the thought comes again. What you've thought about once surfaces again some time or

GEORG SCHWALM-THEISS

"Of course it is the site. I mean, it really says something."

other. It's good when you are not under pressure and are able to turn an idea over in your mind, things worked out hastily aren't really so good."

Schwalm-Theiss, grandson of Siegfried Theiss, is a partner in the oldest firm of architects in Vienna. Founded in 1907 by Siegfried Theiss and Hans Jaksch, for the first five years the office was located at no. 35 Tigergasse in Vienna's eight district. The wish for more greenery and less city noise — the first children had been born in both the Theiss and Jaksch families — led to office moving to the exclusive perimeter of the city. From 1912 onwards without interruption the architects' office has been located in a building erected around that time at no. 21 Altgasse, not far from Schönbrunn Palace, still the imperial summer residence when the practice was set up. Hans Jaksch's son, Walter Jaksch, became a partner in the firm in 1954 and worked there almost until his death at the age of 90. In 1972 Horst Gressenbauer, who remained in the firm until 2008, as well as Theophil Melichar, started work there. Georg Schwalm-Theiss, the grandson of Siegfried Theiss, joined the office in 1976. In 2007 Alfons Bresich became a partner.

GEORG SCHWALM-THEISS

"I need the simultaneous, I find the sequential way things are presented on the monitor difficult."

SCHWALM-THEISS & STUDIES SCHOOL EXTENSION STADT HAAG, PLANNING 2000–2001

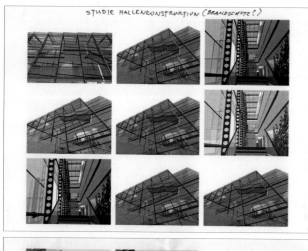
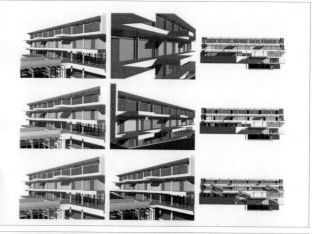

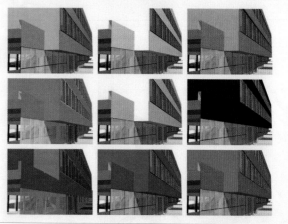

FIGURES: SCHWALM-THEISS & BRESICH

Although this firm has been in continuous existence for 101 years not a single historic photograph of the office rooms has survived. "Not so many photographs were taken. But there are photos of construction sites where the founders of the office can be seen. There is a portrait photo of the pair," emphasises Georg Schwalm-Theiss, who worked through the plan and photograph archive of the office for his dissertation that appeared under the title "Theiss und Jaksch Architekten 1907–1961". "A great deal was thrown away." Although there still exist plan books kept in chronological order, and all the plans were continuously numbered, the development processes cannot be mapped out in any detail. Design work on the high-rise building in Herrengasse started in May 1930 and most likely sketches were made but not a single one has survived. Schwalm-Theiss suspects that "they made a direct start on drawing the plans". In the plan book the first plans for the high-rise building are dated May 26, 1930 and, even at this early development stage, are marked by a high degree of definition, and a finalised, well thought-out quality. Despite the precise entries in the plan book it is impossible to tell who drew which plans. Schwalm-Theiss attributes a number of sheets with distinctively different lettering to Bernard Rudolfsky, who worked in the office of Theiss-Jaksch between 1930 and 1932. Schwalm-Theiss can still remember the wooden frames in which the diazo paper was stretched and the transparent tracing paper original placed over it. By laying them on the broad projecting external windowsill the prints were developed directly by sunlight. The typical smell of ammonia is equally unforgettable. He is also certain that for a long time there was in the office one of those large wooden dividers that architects took with them when visiting the construction site, but like all the other formerly indispensable architectural tools he can recall, this too has not survived. Dr. Alfred Lechner, for many years head of the

THE PRINTS WERE DEVELOPED DIRECTLY BY SUNLIGHT.

GEORG SCHWALM-THEISS

"You can't fudge anything with the computer."

archive at the Vienna University of Technology, still remembers the white work coat that he wore when a member of staff in the office of Theiss-Jaksch. Today he still owns one of these coats, typically worn by architects at work.

In talking to Georg Schwalm-Theiss the word "pleasant" crops up repeatedly. Schwalm-Theiss worked as an intern in the studio of Alvar Aalto in the 1960s — a 16mm film he made in Helsinki about the studio was projected onto the white courtyard wall envisaged by Aalto as part of an academy where films and slide shows would be shown — and he recalls that the atmosphere in the office was pleasant. This is also what he wants for the staff in his own office. Pleasantness is also one of the most important sources of inspiration for the design process. This is the quality that should be achieved for users, above all in the area of housing, he believes. "So that things are pleasant for them," says Schwalm-Theiss. "Inspiration is everything. The trees, the water, the sun. The last forty years of life."

GEORG SCHWALM-THEISS

"The trees, the water, the sun ..."

THEISS & JAKSCH, HIGHRISE-BUILDING HERRENGASSE
EMERGENCY STAIRCASE, ISOMETRY UND AXOMETRY 1931

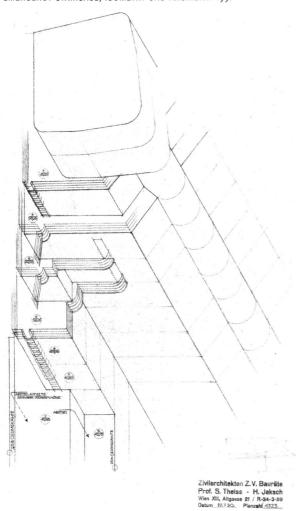

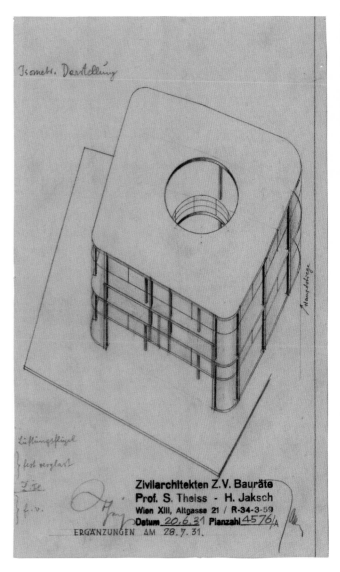

HIGHRISE-BUILDING HERRENGASSE, SITE

"They made a direct start on drawing the plans."

Golden wastepaper baskets

Karl Schwanzer 1918–1975

Atelier Schwanzer 1947–1975
Seilerstätte 16, Seilergasse 16
Vienna
Austria

Field research in the Karl Schwanzer archive in August 2008
conversation with Martin Schwanzer & text: Elke Krasny

The brilliant idea, conceived in loneliness was not Karl Schwanzer's thing. Quite the contrary: through his persistance and passion he and his staff elevated the act of designing to the level of intensive research. His son Martin Schwanzer compares design work in Schwanzer's studio (which was located at number 16 Seilergasse in Vienna) with laboratory research work in the field of the natural sciences in which new series of experiments are constantly set up in order to arrive at the solution to a question. "Painstaking, searching, driven" is how he describes the design method there, a creative process with a scientific approach that presented innumerable "series of experiments" in the form of sketches or models, and by subsequently analysing them, by intuitive recognition, and by comparing them side by side selected the right, the appropriate solution. "But every attempt to advance into unknown territory demands the courage to accept the incomplete, as well as the will to achieve something better. The notion of something being complete is an arrogant one, as it suggests a conclusion and there is no area of human life where there is not room for improvement." (SCHWANZER 1973: 4) The belief that improvement was always possible was a constant incentive to think ideas further and to test things, which made it impossible to use time in an economical way or to shorten the process, and led to a passionate, obsessively heightened "iterative search" that would then allow the decision to be made. This process of "varieties" (CF. FEUERSTEIN IN SCHWANZER 1973: 19) was not preceded by the idea of something concrete, the convinced development of a fixed concept, instead the decision was one possible final stroke that resulted from a work process characterised by many other, additional possibilities. Ideas of the most different kinds were tested, sketches were ceaselessly made and equally regularly discarded. This obsessive working the problem through, the use of repetition as a mode of change reveals an immensely extravagant approach to the creative process. In this context Martin Schwanzer speaks of "golden wastepaper baskets." Günther Feuerstein, who worked in Schwanzer's studio from 1958 to 1962, recalls that they drew "many different variations on large amounts of butter paper. Schwanzer came along, saw — and filled the wastepaper basket." (FEUERSTEIN IN SCHWANZER 1973: 18)

Schwanzer himself drew little. When he did, he frequently used thick felt pens that were, in fact, difficult to hold and which his son Martin compares with a small bottle of Tipp-ex (correction fluid). These thick felt pens lay in the hand more like a stylus than a brush. "In comparison to others Schwanzer drew in a cheeky way." But the medium most essentially his own was not the drawing but the ability to conduct, to direct. In "producing" he really "came

PHOTOS: MARTIN SCHWANZER

MARTIN SCHWANZER

"Architecture was my father's plaything, with which he could run riot, it wasn't work in the sense of slaving away, but a kind of diversion."

into his own". Consequently, Karl Schwanzer did not screen-off an area of the studio for design work, his desk stood alongside the others in the drafting office. The "handcrafts room" for model building was also "in the middle of the office". Until the 1960s white coats were worn, the staff "smeared all over the place, working with graphite, and erased again". Although every project from the studio, "almost every design" was a "Schwanzer" (FEUERSTEIN IN SCHWANZER 1973: 18), the hierarchy in the office was a matter of constant negotiation between the staff. "It was easy to rearrange the pyramid," says Martin Schwanzer. Small teams of four to five members of staff — all trained architects or students of architecture, no technical draughtsmen — concentrated on a project. At times two teams tackled the same project, as competitors. Which member of the team would direct the project was decided by a process of negotiation involving group dynamics. Schwanzer's own "wrestling for a solution," the striving for "wit," for "quality," permeated the office atmosphere as a constantly present expectation. Rüdiger Lainer has coined the term "creative absence" for this kind of staff motivation. During work on competitions "things were pretty wild," at the working drawings stage things were done like in a building contractor's office, with details and specifications. Then things were stricter." Martin Schwanzer sees this as "two different worlds," that is, office

KARL SCHWANZER

"The idea of reducing stress is inconceivable in a creative profession."

COMPETITION DESIGN AUSTRIAN PAVILION EXPO '67 MONTRÉAL

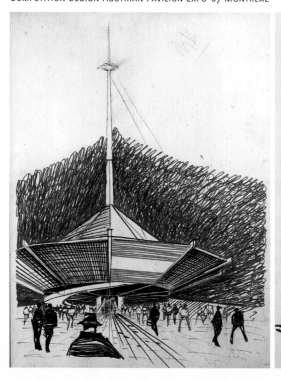

and studio in one. "Economic solutions may meet the needs, but whether they fulfil them is another question." (SCHWANZER 1973: 11) Economy as a restriction, a corset, is burst open, not only in his buildings but also in his individual way of working, which was committed to the abundance of extravagance as a solution and to a search that essentially can never be ended as a creative motor. "Not being able to stop during the development phase of a design can end up as a kind of manic obsession. Not always to the delight of those most affected in the architect's immediate surroundings." (SCHWANZER 1973: 7)

Hitting "the nerve of an era," taking in the "cultural atmosphere"– these were important for his approach to "producing". The main concern was always the "message," how something "can be best conveyed". In his commitment to a design that he believed in Karl Schwanzer could go very far indeed. To convince the BMW shareholders and managers about his design for BMW building in Munich (that he ultimately carried out) he invested over one and half million Austrian shillings out of his own pocket. Stageset carpenters in the Bavaria Studios in Geiselgasteig made a round segment of the high-rise building, painted around the windows the distant view of the silhouette of Munich looking towards the Alps including the already completed Olympic Games grounds, set up office furniture and typewriters, recorded office

AFTER THE COMPETITION A SERIES OF STUDY MODELS LED TO A WHOLE NEW DESIGN.
GEOMETRIC STUDY MODELS AUSTRIAN PAVILION EXPO '67 MONTRÉAL

PHOTOS: ATELIER SCHWANZER

MARTIN SCHWANZER ABOUT HIS FATHER

"Architecture can also be spoken."

sounds and dressed up 30 extras in business suits. But all this expenditure, which ultimately led to a successful arrangement on December 2, 1968, was only undertaken because Schwanzer had recognised that conventional methods of communicating architecture to the client, i.e. models, plans and discussions, were not adequate to allow the possibility become reality.

The tirelessly industrious Schwanzer, who also spent many weekends working in his office, drew his inspiration from his travels and from art. Working together and talking to "painters, sculptors, with Hoflehner, with Wotruba" was "the greatest fun". He had "subscriptions to magazines, was very well-read". When he travelled abroad he wanted to know from others what interesting, new things there were to be seen. After the Second World War Schwanzer actively sought the exchange of ideas with the international architecture public, was curious about the world. "Then came the first trips abroad. Paris, Zurich, Canada. Paris, despite the post-war shortages a magnificent, stimulating, generous city, was for me overwhelming, as all I had before was cities in ruins." As professor at the Vienna University of Technology, where Schwanzer worked from 1959 to 1975, he placed emphasis on looking at architecture, on becoming familiar with current trends, new technological possibilities and cultural situations, which he had always found so stimulating. With his students he went on

KARL SCHWANZER

"My staff have shown great patience with me in bearing with my temperament and my restlessness."

STUDY MODELS AUSTRIAN PAVILION EXPO '67 MONTRÉAL

trips to Berlin, Paris, and in 1964 to the USA. Schwanzer laid emphasis on the method of "stimulation by absence," not only in his studio but also in the institute. But he made time for the end-of-term corrections and produced pages of handwritten comments. Many of his students, such as Laurids Ortner, Wolf D. Prix, Boris Podrecca or Heinz Neumann later worked for him. In the studio Schwanzer allowed the staff to develop ideas. Then he had them present their concepts, assessed them and distributed approvals. "Every project consists of a highly individual, non-conformist approach."

REFERENCE
Schwanzer, Karl (1973) Architektur aus Leidenschaft. Wien, München: modulverlag.

STRUCTURE UND FINAL MODEL AUSTRIAN PAVILION EXPO '67 MONTRÉAL

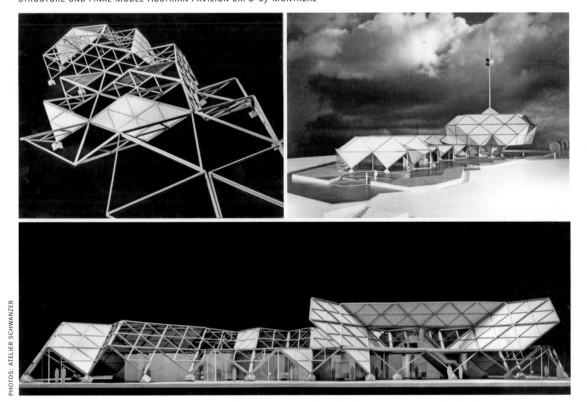

PHOTOS: ATELIER SCHWANZER

LAURIDS ORTNER
"His impulsiveness both destroys rationalisation plans and hurls worked-out designs into the wastepaper basket."

We do not do paper architecture

SOM

Skidmore, Owings & Merill LLP
224 South Michigan Avenue #1000
Chicago
USA

Field research in the office in January 2007
interview and email correspondence with
Colin Franzen & text Elke Krasny

For decades the architecture firm of Skidmore, Owings & Merrill LLP, founded in 1936, has had its office opposite the Chicago Art Museum, with a view of Lake Michigan. SOM, a globally active architecture firm, has branches in nine cities, including – alongside Chicago – New York, San Francisco, London, Los Angeles, Washington DC, Hong Kong, Shanghai and Brussels. The total number of staff worldwide is 1,600. The acronym SOM precisely embodies the original idea of this firm's founders: not to tie the making of architecture to a charismatic figure, not to attribute the work of many to a single creator, the author of the architecture, but to understand and to publish the creative process of architecture as a matter for the company as a whole. The founders focused on developing an organisational model for an architecture firm and saw making architecture as a creative process that takes place within a clearly structured hierarchy. Down to the present day the shaping of work by the group has remained a decisive factor that is expressed in the studio-based organisational principle of the firm.

Colin Franzen, one of the staff of the Chicago office which has a staff of 500, functioned as the tour guide in January 2007. He describes the high degree of communication and networking between the various international office locations. "All the partners meet monthly. At the upper level there is a great deal of communication between the offices." The partners discuss current projects, orientation for the future, and the strategic development of the firm. But discussions are not confined to the partners, there is also communication and exchange of ideas between the individual offices at different degrees of intensity "There are people from Chicago in London right now."

"The organization is very fluid. We move around as the demand grows, like baseball players who get traded. We are 500 people and we get constantly shuffled around. You might not know today where you will be next week." The spatial organisation of the Chicago office serves to intensify the collaboration between the various specialised planning disciplines in their respective studios. In the course of any one project the make-up of the team can change frequently and is flexibly adapted to the respective work phases as the project progresses. The sophisticated management of staff resources – there is a separate personnel department – is clearly reflected in the spatial structuring of the organisation. Design teams are grouped and work with one another in cubicles that are separated from each other by space dividers. When the team expands more desks are simply moved into the generously sized cubicles. "More people move in."

PHOTOS: SOM

Colin Franzen

"We currently have about 100 active projects in the office."

Whereas up to a few years ago the importance and prestige of one's position within the firm's hierarchy was expressed by a suitably large corner office, at best with a view of the lake, today the changes in the firm's philosophy are demonstrated by the fact that, during the redesign in 2006, these corner offices were defined as general meeting rooms. Colin Franzen explains: "When they rebuilt the office, they levelled the hierarchy. The project managers are on the floor with everybody else. Who is an intern and who is an architect, you can't tell."

In many of their competition entries and also in other international projects visiting the building site, i.e. the physical analysis of the site at the start of the project, is simply not feasible. Often the start of a new project is a kind of beginning at a distance, imagining and developing in the office, far away from the actual building site. "We start abstractly, not from the site. Most of the time we work from the distance." But increasingly the examination of the cultural usages of a country presents a challenge for the global production of architecture by SOM, a challenge that it is difficult to resolve with tightly organised timetables — the average duration of a project is fourteen months. However, allowing more time for research into the culture of the respective country and the study of local building traditions is regarded as desirable. "We are an international firm, we do have to examine why forms look the way they do."

Today the intensive study of new technologies as well as constant reflection on the tools as the means in creative and economic use is characteristic of the way SOM works as a firm, and historically this has always been the case. Major importance is attached to collaboration at the level of staff resources, but also to the exploitation of technological possibilities. Walter Netch used the computer, back then enormous mainframe computers, to carry out his field theory experiments. Faz Kahn wrote his own special software for structural calculations. Traditionally this firm is characterised by the strategic expansion of the tools used for making architecture and by an understanding of technology as an advanced and driving productive force in the design process.

COLIN FRANZEN

"We have approximately 500 employees in the Chicago office."

MODELS NORTH BUND TOWER WHITE MAGNOLIA PLAZA, SHANGHAI   CROWN-AERIAL

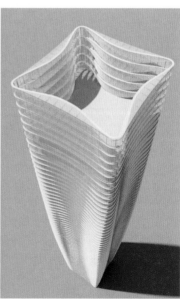

PHOTOS: SOM

While this year, for the new NATO headquarters in Brussels, the Chicago office is using BIM (Building information Modeling) for the first time in a project of this size, back in the mid-1980s SOM already produced its own software that could do much the same, and was one of the pioneers in the development of CAD for architects. AES, Architectural and Engineering Series, is the name of the command controlled programme developed by SOM that was also used to model in 3D. Developing the firm's own software, a strategy typical for the industry, was applied to the production of architecture. In the mid-1980s people at SOM were working on mainframe computers with the DRAFT system, which was VAX-based and used Tektronix terminals. The work method based on the collaboration of a number of specialist disciplines was directly expressed in the software developed by SOM, as it could be used by different specialist planners at the same time and facilitated communication between them. Today five different disciplines work together in the Chicago office: "architects, interior designers, mechanical engineers, structural engineers and urban planners." The flow of information between all the disciplines involved is essential — and this applies to both verbal and digital communication. In Building Information Modeling, which is tested at a large scale, it is precisely this form of transverse information management along all the specialist planning disciplines involved that crops up, an aspect that was decisive in the development of the firm's own software, AES.

"The more we work on it, the more I can feel the digital space," Franzen describes the way in which expertise in digital and digitalised perception of space is gradually becoming standard. "I don't make 3D prints. I have a feeling of what is in the computer. We are cooking

FIGURES: SOM

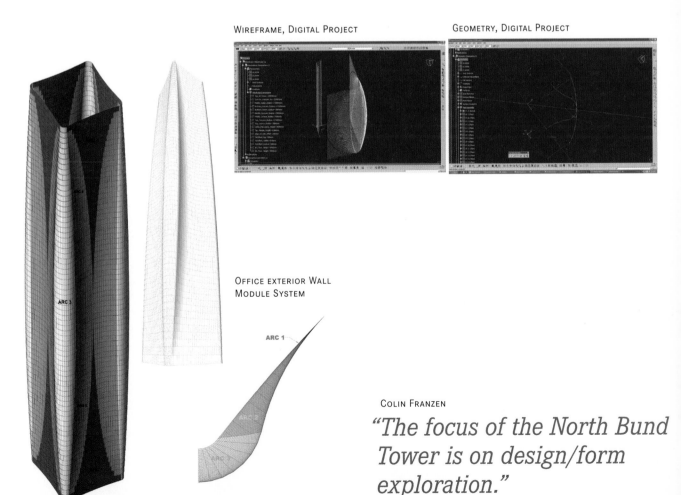

WIREFRAME, DIGITAL PROJECT

GEOMETRY, DIGITAL PROJECT

OFFICE EXTERIOR WALL MODULE SYSTEM

ARC 1

COLIN FRANZEN

"The focus of the North Bund Tower is on design/form exploration."

up new things all the time," he emphasises, although the CAD library would allow them to take a different approach. "We never build the same curtain wall facade twice." They have been using Digital Project, a parametric project lifecycle management developed by Gehry Technologies that combines Building Information Modeling with Catia, since 2006. Technology plays a decisive role in terms of feasibility between the crystallization of form and construction.

"Digital tools are informing new shapes. Now we have the digital production to actually make the shapes. We push the engineers to get the forms real." Whereas Burj Dubai, the world's tallest building, stands for the engineering, technical and construction-oriented sides of the office, they are at the same time experimenting with parametric software for both design and production. "Most interestingly, we are now pioneering efforts to combine the intelligence of these tools, Catia's design potential with Revit's production capabilities, as well as allowing the environment to inform the design through a host of newly scripted tools."

In their day-to-day work designing with the technological possibilities is decisive. "Your daily task is that you are no longer drawing, you are building, physically constructing a building." Whereas with AutoCAD the method of working at the computer had "the same logic as the drafting board — operating in 2 dimensions," now the "move into 3D" is taking place. Although within the office starting off can take very different forms — for example with sketches or work models — development in 3D and communication in 3D are characteristic

THREE DIFFERENT GEOMETRIES OF THE BURJ DUBAI WERE TESTED, EACH WITH VARIOUS STRUCTURAL PROPERTIES, TO PREDICT THE WIND-INDUCED BASE LOADS AND ACCELERATIONS AT THE TOP OCCUPIED FLOORS OF THE TOWER.

STRUCTURAL MODEL AT 1:500 (LEFT)
29" HIGH BY 6" RADIUS AT BASE
STRUCTURAL MODEL AT 1:500 (RIGHT)
58" HIGH AND 7" RADIUS AT BASE

MODELLE DES BURJ DUBAI: GEOMETRISCHE FORMFINDUNG, ABGELEITET AUS WINDSTUDIEN

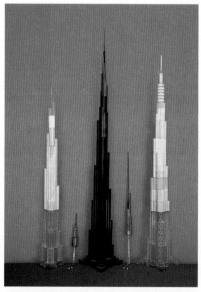

FIGURES: SOM

of the development process, not just in the computer but also using physically built models, examples of which are found throughout the office. In the workshop, alongside the model builders and a considerable number of interns, you can come across architects or partners who want to try out something directly, physically, with their hands or to check something quickly. "A partner will say: build me a model. If you can't build a model, you can't build a building. We don't do paper architecture. We get out of paper architecture."

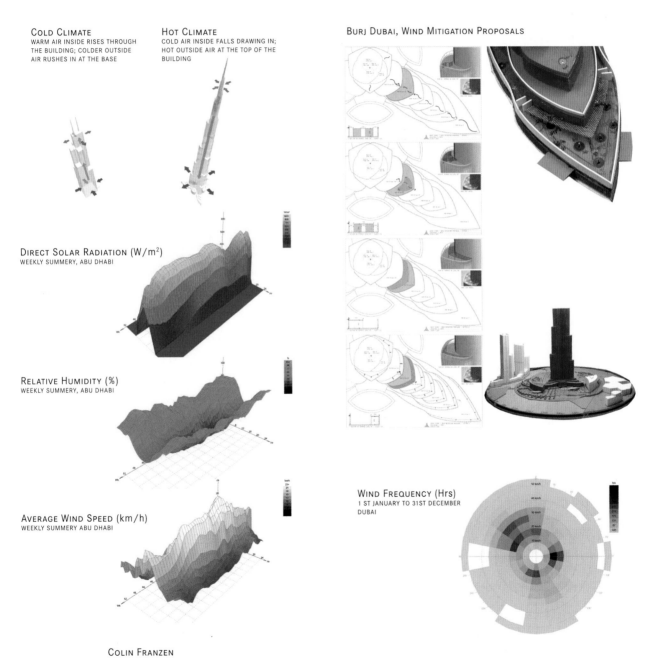

COLD CLIMATE
WARM AIR INSIDE RISES THROUGH THE BUILDING; COLDER OUTSIDE AIR RUSHES IN AT THE BASE

HOT CLIMATE
COLD AIR INSIDE FALLS DRAWING IN; HOT OUTSIDE AIR AT THE TOP OF THE BUILDING

BURJ DUBAI, WIND MITIGATION PROPOSALS

DIRECT SOLAR RADIATION (W/m²)
WEEKLY SUMMERY, ABU DHABI

RELATIVE HUMIDITY (%)
WEEKLY SUMMERY, ABU DHABI

AVERAGE WIND SPEED (km/h)
WEEKLY SUMMERY ABU DHABI

WIND FREQUENCY (Hrs)
1 ST JANUARY TO 31ST DECEMBER DUBAI

COLIN FRANZEN

"The technical (structural and construction) achievements are highlighted on Burj."

Tools are everything

UNStudio

STADHOUDERSKADE 113
AMSTERDAM
THE NETHERLANDS

FIELD RESEARCH IN THE STUDIO IN DECEMBER 2006
PHOTOGRAPHY, INTERVIEW WITH BEN VAN BERKEL
& TEXT ELKE KRASNY

"I really like to use tools. I celebrate tools and design techniques," says architect Ben van Berkel, who in 1999 founded UNStudio with art historian Caroline de Bos. Van Berkel & Bos Architectuur Bureau, which had worked in Amsterdam since 1988, launched a well-prepared internal reorganisation and international expansion shortly before the beginning of the new millennium. The name suggests their programme. UNStudio stands for United Network for Urbanism, Infrastructure and Architecture. Efficient, professional and creative the office functions as a studio, laboratory, factory and club that is characterised by a kind of plug-in professionalism .

The transformation was accompanied by a theoretical manifesto. Maximum leeway for creativity correlates with exploiting the computer's potential, and with strategic management. The three volumes of Move appeared in 1999. The formulation of theory in writing is an integral part of the production. "Move was written as a manifesto. An ideal way of setting up a studio. We published Move, the book came out and we set up the studio like this, it was part of the book. It was an interactive, actual process, actual not virtual. We make things and bring theory into it. Not after-theory."

Smart practitioners of the architectural profession with years of experience under their belt work alongside with young graduates who studied in Columbia or Harvard, international experts and consultants with local firms. "If I had to draw a diagram to show how we are structured, it wouldn't be an easy diagram to draw, it would be a satellite diagram." The creative processes are accelerated both technologically and in terms of organisation and are constantly made more professional. "I learned 15 years ago to hire the best specialists and to pay them the best salaries."

A staff of 80, 25 of them from Holland, 55 of international origins, work in flexible design teams of between five and six persons. "Design-wise we keep teams small. When a project runs, there are seven to eight people in a design team." The project architect in charge is called the caretaker. "The design team is a floating platform that is not so clearly defined. You can't fix quality at the design phase, you can't force the unexpected." Design, planning, human resources, organisation, communication and cost management are interlocked as closely as possible and organised in platforms. Since 2001 the firm has had its own quality management, which is based on international management standards in accordance with the ISO 9001 guidelines. "We have project team members and caretakers. We split the external communication between Caroline and myself. We have a coordination team of three per

BEN VAN BERKEL

"We make things and bring theory into it. Not after-theory."

project, with one member from the management." The idea of the "master-builder" is completely outdated. "As an architect you need to be a public scientist. You have to create your own system of dialogues with every part of your bits, this allows for new insights in communication." The innovative aspect lies in the production of architecture as the dynamic management of knowledge, which places all elements in relationship to each other at as early a stage as possible. "Guiding is my only talent," says van Berkel. UNStudio is a network as an inner office structure. "I am super speculative. I like to speculate, and mix people together. I believe in the intelligence of the office. The architect is like John Cage between the orchestra."

The architecture production laboratory of UNStudio is housed in a narrow four-storey building. "The organisation of a building is more important than its style." This applies to their own office, too. When work continues through the night people sometimes sleep on a sofa designed by UNStudio, there is a table football awaiting players, on Thursdays they all have lunch together. "The partners meet every Monday to discuss major organizational aspects. On Friday we have design reviews with people from outside." The network includes clients, investors, management experts, specialists, structural engineers, designers and stylists. The taylorised architecture laboratory attempts to make the traditional creative flair of a studio possible; efficient organisation does not inevitably exclude socialising in a party mood. "We had to physically change, get a new jacket. It was once more like an artist's atelier, now it is

VILLA NM, UPSTATE NEW YORK 2000–2006; DESIGN: BEN VAN BERKEL WITH OLAF GIPSER AND ANDREW BENN, COLETTE PARRAS, JACCO VAN WENGERDEN, MARIA EUGENIA DIAZ, JAN DEBELIUS, MARTIN KUITERT, PABLO RICA, OLGA VAZQUEZ-RUANO; LOCAL CONSULTANT: ROEMER PIERIK

more professional. But socially it is still an atelier. We do lunches with clients, we do Friday drinks." Spaces for communication are created when members of staff meet each other on the landings of the narrow staircase and discuss new issues such as future collaboration in the design team. At the closely placed desks the chairs are moved together to one side to create a meeting space. In addition to Dutch you hear German, or English. The model construction workshop is at ground floor level along with part of the archive, two other relocated archives contain models, plans and correspondence from the era before emails.

Ben van Berkel's work area is separated from the architecture production hall. His small room emanates the atmosphere of a globalised nomadic worker who hardly ever sits at his desk (which has no computer) but hurries through the office, guiding discussions and tirelessly pursuing his managerial responsibilities. A mini-library including twelve colourful Domus volumes (Domus 1930s–1990s: The Very Best from the Seminal Architecture and Design Journal 1928–1999), a narrow desk without a mess of papers, a laptop packed in its travelling case, and a few sketches on the wall behind the desk make up the rudimentary furnishings. "I open my mind to what surrounds me. I do a lot of sketching before sleeping. It is very strict behaviour, how to make ideas, how to come up with the idea for the next day." Sketching is the techne of creative production. "I do a lot of sketching when flying. I paint a lot. I love to sit down in the evening breaks to paint." He uses whatever is available. "I sketch with everything, not only the pencil, I sketch with the brush, or with pencil. I tear a piece of

BEN VAN BERKEL

"I don not really get my inspiration so much on paper. I do not show the sketches. I communicate by words. The paintings are my secret observations."

paper, I really like to use tools." The design process is a communicative practice within a team. "We design in a team. I do not really get my inspiration so much on paper. I do not show the sketches. I communicate by words. The paintings are my secret observations." Designing means making decisions. "It is like in music, you make your own notes, and you rewrite them continuously, by re-listening." Teaching provides a model for a way of working based on communication. "Teaching is one of my most important inspirations. When it came to setting up dialogue, I developed my own system at the Staedel School. Let them learn how to develop their own tools, their own thinking." Communication is the key to the design process. "We have an incredible dialogue culture. I promote that culture a lot. The most difficult aspect is communication. Tidying up with the infrastructure of communication."

The increasing acceleration caused by the computer exerts pressure on the design process. "We try to be as compact as possible. In the first phases of the design we already start with the engineering and the cost principles. With the computer it is possible to design

BEN VAN BERKEL'S SKETCHES FOR THE VILLA NM

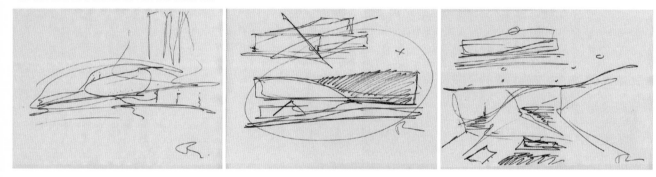

BEN VAN BERKEL UND CAROLINE DE BOS

"The conceptual model for VilLA NM is a box with a blob-like moment in the middle; a twist in both plan and section that causes a simple shoebox to bifurcate into two separate, split-level volumes."

VILLA NM, UPSTATE NEW YORK 2000—2006; VOLUMETRIC ORGANISATION

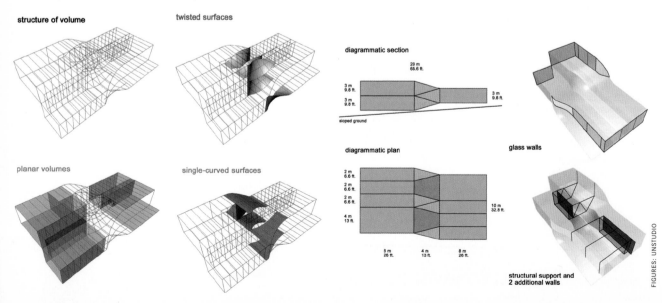

FIGURES: UNSTUDIO

in such a short time. We have developed the tools of animating geometric models. We can do 50 changes in a day. We animate it in a day, do a 3D model and each local change corrects itself in 10 minutes."

In much the same way that directing staff is essential, directing the intelligent tool that is the computer is also important. "Tools could give a new insight. Tools could change the way of looking at things." Ben van Berkel is fascinated and inspired by tools and their potential. The important thing is to explore the limits of tools, to help their creativity develop. "If you look at the history of art, it is tools, experimenting with tools that made a difference. Seurat and pointillism for example, colour photography let us rethink how we paint the image. It was about expanding the image." Today the issue is the expansion of architecture by exploiting the tools available to the utmost. "There is a seemingly unlimited amount of possibilities. We know the limitations of form-making. We are taking it to the most extreme form."

The issue is not celebrating the generation of form. "I take great care to guide the computer. We are not only interested in design techniques. We want to know how to guide the design and develop experimental design techniques."

Whereas previously diagrams provided guideline images for design, now it is "the guiding process. We call the maps models of thinking. It is about the moment of capturing ideas. The use of mathematical models guides your relational aspects much better." Van Berkel criticises the computer fascination and obsession with form of many of his colleagues. "How can you develop a new, fully integral way of making objects? We try to develop a prototypical system. The most important thing is to filter and edit. The computer is so rich, you have to use it as a clever editing tool. You have to make your choices, learn and think. We have to develop new concepts of control, not a linear system, but contemporary techniques that think of relational compositions. I am more like an artist than an architect. Architects celebrate the exterior far too much. They use tools in the wrong manner. It is not only about form-making. The computer is an intelligent machine. Architects should use the intelligence of the machine."

Ben van Berkel

"Architects celebrate the exterior far too much."

The glory of mess

VSBA Venturi Scott Brown & Associates

4236 MAIN STREET
MANYANK
PHILADELPHIA
USA

FIELD RESEARCH IN THE OFFICE IN JANUARY 2007
PHOTOGRAPHY, CONVERSATIONS WITH DENISE SCOTT BROWN,
JOHN IZENOUR, NANCY ROGO TRAINER, JAMES KOLKER, DANIEL MACCOUBREY,
JEREMY TENENBAUM AND SUSAN SCANLON & TEXT: ELKE KRASNY

"We work on the weekend. People in the office don't see how we work together. It happens when no one is around," says Denise Scott Brown explaining the artistic work processes involved in her 'joint artistry' with Robert Venturi. "Ideas can spring from two minds. It is a fusion of minds."

After various changes of members the office set up by Robert Venturi in 1960, in which Denise Scott Brown has been a partner since 1967, has operated under the title Venturi Scott Brown and Associates since 1989. Today this office is characterised by an attempt to achieve a delicate balance between change and continuity. The acronym VSBA — which is gradually becoming the firm's name — represents an identity that is in a state of change. "Clients don't trust old people," complains Scott Brown.

Venturi and Scott Brown originally shared an office and since that time she is used to having to organise herself in a tiny space. She writes her carefully edited texts — which strive for precise formulations while avoiding the use of specialist jargon and include offers to clients, reports on campus designs, lectures, and essays — "in a kind of cubbyhole". "Writing is a tool with clients, but it also explains our ideas to colleagues from the world." Closely packed grey volumes contain lectures from her time as a teacher, lectures from the last six or seven years exist only on the computer. From the drawer of a brown roll-top desk Denise Scott Brown takes out tools filled with memories. "The last form of drafting I did was with Rapidograph. This is part of my bones. It gives me a history, now I use pencils a lot. These are my mother's compasses, dated 1928. She gave them to me. These are my first husband's compasses from 1948. Now, I love my BlackBerry, I use the computer, the dictaphone, the pencil, a mix of things."

Whereas Denise Scott Brown needs seclusion, Robert Venturi's desk is at the centre of things. The staff explain that "Bob is in the drafting room rather than in an office," as this better suits his openness and accessibility. Robert Venturi's desk (which doesn't have a computer on it) almost vanishes beneath a heap of objets trouvés, references from the history of art or architecture, small tools, coloured Post-It notes — a random collection of colourful visual material and objects filled with life. The three principals, Nancy Rogo Trainer, James Kolker and Daniel MacCoubrey refer to his talent as a draughtsman: "Bob always rekindled the development of the drafting vocabulary of the office."

At the beginning, Denise Scott Brown explains, "computational design was the coefficient of simulation available, now that's the last thing you need." Since the mid-1980s work in the office has been carried out as a hybrid mix of hand and computer drawings. In conversation

DENISE SCOTT BROWN AND ROBERT VENTURI,
TSINGHUA UNIVERSITY CAMPUS IN PEKING.

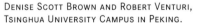

DENISE SCOTT BROWN

*"We are hardly
a corporate firm."*

with the principals the remark is made that "we are now entering into 3D computer world. There is so much sophistication required in renderings, but it is more expectation than needs." Rolls of yellow trace, fineliners, black ink, coloured markers are used for the design process. On a large light table various proposals drawn on tracing paper are laid on top each other, compared with each other. "Wait a second, let's sketch on top of it, that'll give us a broader range of options," says a member of staff.

"For a long time we had all the computers in one dark room. Then in one huge bold move we moved the computers out of the computer room and allocated a computer to each person." Comparisons were made between what the computer can do and the individual expressive power of hand drawing or hand colouring. "You can transfer these qualities to the computer, but not the subtleties," Scott Brown says. Nancy Rogo Trainer, James Kolker and Daniel MacCoubrey find that computer generated drawings are "too precise too early. With the computer the drawings looked finished before we were finished." Nowadays the software Squiggle provides the effects of drawings made by hand. "Leaving things incomplete is a strong inspiration, not to strive for too much perfection." Denise Scott Brown believes that what counts is the potential of the incomplete, rather than the appearance of hyper-perfection.

NANCY ROGO TRAINER

"Bob always rekindled the development of the drafting vocabulary of the office."

ROBERT VENTURI'S SKETCHES, EPISCOPAL ACADEMY PHILADELPHIA, 2004 (2008 UNDER CONSTRUCTION)

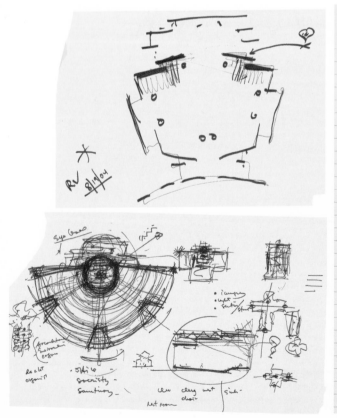

"We are hardly a corporate firm. We have another approach here. There is a difference between earning a living and leading a life. We lead a life in architecture."

In 1981 the firm moved from central Philadelphia to Manyank, a kind of in-between area where the city meets suburbia. "We fell in love with the building. We drew a deep breath and took it," Denise Scott Brown recalls. The shop front is designed to communicate projects or statements to the Main Street. Models are built at ground floor level, one floor higher are the workplaces of Nancy Rogo Trainer, James Kolker and Daniel MacCoubrey and the other members of the staff. The reception area, a large meeting room, Bob's desk, Denise's cubbyhole as well as cubicles for the staff are on the second floor. The long history of the office in the form of sketches, plans, models, slides, collected objects, and publications is spreading upwards into the loft space. Just like in her campus designs — "I might be the last person left using it," says Denise Scott Brown — where the interaction of the existing and its potential is of central importance, the office is characterised by an interplay of the formal and informal. "There are formal and informal rituals. Every Monday morning we have a job development meeting from 9 am to 11 am. In counterpoint to that constant informal meetings take place in passing by a desk or in meeting at a lunch table," explains staff member Jeremy Tenenbaum.

"Bob is in the drafting room rather than in an office."

The design teams are small, each one works on a project from start to finish. This ensures detailed knowledge and allows all decisions to be traced back to a specific point in the process. There is an intensive exchange of opinions with the project managers. Robert Venturi and the respective project manager discuss the large projects once a week. "Any time they want to they can talk with us, we are a small enough office," the three principals say with one voice, explaining the communication structures. Generally three staff members work together at the start of a design, then between five and six in a team. Concentrated work phases help to crystallise ideas. "Charrettes are like workshops, think-tanks for a day." Denise Scott Brown recalls that her longest period "in conclave" lasted 65 hours. "We don't work that hard any more, you have to stop to smell the roses," she says these days.

The ideas are developed through a process of discussing and sketching them in which the semantic historical and topographical contexts are decisive. "The glory of clutter, the glory of mess." The large meeting room is like a visiting card: the chairs have returned from an

DENISE SCOTT BROWN

"I might be the last person left using this method of campus design."

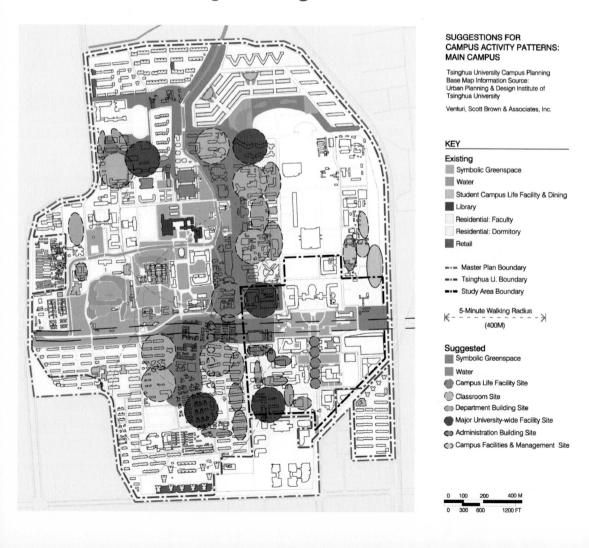

SUGGESTIONS FOR CAMPUS ACTIVITY PATTERNS: MAIN CAMPUS

Tsinghua University Campus Planning
Base Map Information Source:
Urban Planning & Design Institute of
Tsinghua University

Venturi, Scott Brown & Associates, Inc.

KEY

Existing

- Symbolic Greenspace
- Water
- Student Campus Life Facility & Dining
- Library
- Residential: Faculty
- Residential: Dormitory
- Retail

- Master Plan Boundary
- Tsinghua U. Boundary
- Study Area Boundary

5-Minute Walking Radius
(400M)

Suggested

- Symbolic Greenspace
- Water
- Campus Life Facility Site
- Classroom Site
- Department Building Site
- Major University-wide Facility Site
- Administration Building Site
- Campus Facilities & Management Site

0 100 200 400 M
0 300 600 1200 FT

exhibition, the work of VSBA is arranged on the walls in the form of a dense collage. Denise Scott Brown regards the photo-essay as an ideal form of communication.

The design process starts with a discussion with the potential clients. The office does not take part in competitions on principle, as ideas are developed through a process of dialogue with a partner. The issue is not the solution but filtering the possibilities that can be discussed. "We try to get ideas from our clients, we use iconography to reflect the client," says Nancy Rogo Trainer.

Regular visits are made to the potential site, the analysis is then synthesised. "Photographing is part of my personal vision," Denise Scott Brown explains. The concept of "learning from," whether it be from Las Vegas, Tokyo, Shanghai or the Manyank Canal behind their own building resembles the detailed analysis of building sites or campuses. "We remap the map. It is about creative ways to bring together variables of what is needed in a design. What to connect with what. I think in patterns, but I am an architect."

DENISE SCOTT BROWN

"The last form of drafting I did was with Rapidograph. This is part of my bones. It gives me a history."

SNAPSHOTS

LACATON & VASSAL, PHOTO: ELKE KRASNY

STEVEN HOLL ARCHITECTS, PHOTO: GUDRUN HAUSEGGER

LACATON & VASSAL

DILLER SCOFIDIO + RENFRO

YONA FRIEDMAN

VENTURI SCOTT BROWN & ASSOCIATES

ATELIER BOW-WOW

EDGE DESIGN INSTITUTE

THE JERDE PARTNERSHIP

VENTURI SCOTT BROWN & ASSOCIATES

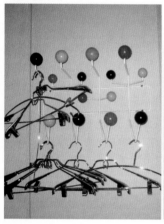

HERMANN CZECH

EDGE DESIGN INSITUTE

THE JERDE PARTNERSHIP

YONA FRIEDMAN

PHOTOS: ELKE KRASNY, GUDRUN HAUSEGGER

YONA FRIEDMAN

R&SIE(N)

DILLER SCOFIDIO + RENFRO

UNSTUDIO

THE JERDE PARTNERSHIP

LACATON & VASSAL

HERMANN CZECH

EDGE DESIGN INSTITUTE

HERMANN CZECH

EDGE DESIGN INSTITUTE

DILLER SCOFIDIO + RENFRO

ATELIER BOW-WOW

PHOTOS: ELKE KRASNY, GUDRUN HAUSEGGER

CABANA, HONG KONG AIRPORT, PHOTO: GARY CHANG

THE JERDE PARTNERSHIP, PHOTO: ELKE KRASNY

TOOL STORIES

The Means and the End

Robert Temel

Architects make tools

Joseph Hardtmuth, house architect of Prince Liechtenstein, was one of the inventors of what still remains the most important design tool, the lead pencil. Like his colleagues Hardmuth was dissatisfied with the poor quality of the pencils available at the time. These were either cut from blocks of graphite or pressed out of pulverised graphite mixed with sulphur and antimony. Both of these types broke easily and were often impure. Consequently, around 1795 (and apparently parallel to each other), the Frenchman, Nicolas-Jacques Conté, and Hardmuth developed a new production method. They had the graphite ground and mixed with clay. This made the pencil not only more homogeneous and stable but the pencils could be also be produced in different degrees of hardness, according to the proportion of clay used (WILHELM 1990; PETROSKI 1995). Since that time the lead pencil has not been developed further in any significant technical sense.

There are still reasons today for architects to develop their own tools. For example in the mid-1980s the architects' office of Skidmore, Owings and Merrill (SOM) developed their own software for computer-aided design (CAD) known as AES (Architectural and Engineering Series), which was a programme series that made 3D modeling possible and was command-directed, allowing people to work very quickly. SOM here followed the example of many industrial concerns that, ten years earlier, had begun to use proprietary software (that is to say software they developed themselves). As it was oriented towards collaborative development and towards the needs of different specialised areas of planning AES anticipated functions that many other CAD programmes included only later. Today, under the name Building Information Modeling (BIM), that is to say digital models equipped with all the information necessary for a building, these are again a focus of interest.

Tools and design

Tools exert a direct influence on ideas and help to determine them. However, it is possible to escape this influence and to shape it. The way in which architects employ digital technologies, the way they shape the interplay between sketch or model and communication in the team and the manner in which ideas are communicated to the client depend upon the results aimed at. Hence the conditions that tools impose upon the act of designing are more proposals rather than constraints, albeit proposals in a market with a limited choice. Architects choose the

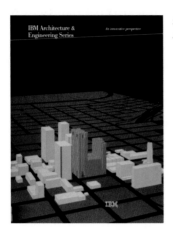

SOM LICENCED THEIR ARCHITECTURAL
AND ENGINEERING SERIES AES TO IBM

tools and methods that can deliver the required result but their choice is influenced in both social and material terms by their personal development and by their particular culture.

For many centuries the tools uses to depict designs remained almost identical – apart, of course, from continuous small technical improvements – whereas over the same period built architecture changed rapidly. Pens with nibs consisting of two pieces of metal that could be adjusted to allow lines of a fixed width to be drawn on paper in India or standard ink existed from classical antiquity to the mid-20th century (NEDOLUHA 1960: 14FF; HAMBLY 1988: 57FF). The technology that then followed, the ink technical pen, essentially did not alter anything, although it made drawing much easier and more comfortable. There were no more problems with dripping ink, cleaning the pens was far simpler and one did not have to constantly adjust the pen to draw strokes of different widths, as there were separate pens for each required width. The first new "Rapidograph" pens were filled with ink like a fountain pen, the tubular nib produced even lines and, unlike the old pens, it did not require great concentration to maintain a constant width and to avoid blotches.

The digital drawing board

The radical change occurred around the end of the 20th century when CAD conquered architects' offices, making both drawing plans by hand and, naturally, also the ink drawing pen, obsolete. People now used a mouse to draw on a monitor that showed digital representations of the classic drawing conventions: floor plans, elevations and sections. The software initially used in architecture came from the motor-car and airplane industries, where the change-over to CAD had been made in the 1970s, but where the interface to material implementation in the form of industrial production functioned considerably better than in the field of architecture. Despite all the progress made in the area of industrialisation building remains by and large based on handcraft and manual labour. Whereas in industrial design digital planning using three-dimensional volume models became standard during the 1980s, for a long time in the field of architecture orthogonal, two-dimensional drawing on the drawing board was simulated in digital space. Later, from the 1990s onwards, when software developments made especially for architecture were already widespread, a new tool made its appearance upon the stage: animation software from the film industry that not only made animated depictions possible but also meant that a variety of geometric operations could be used to explore and discover forms (SCHODEK 2005: 50FF). Together with the expanded

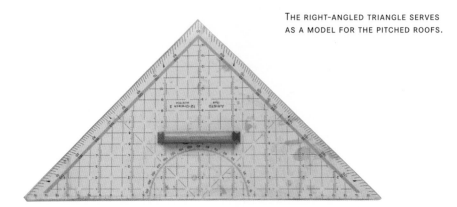

THE RIGHT-ANGLED TRIANGLE SERVES
AS A MODEL FOR THE PITCHED ROOFS.

possibilities for geometrical operations in other CAD programmes this led to the drawing board metaphor on the monitor being abandoned.

From this point onwards when starting to design people no longer drew on the computer but modelled on it, which possibly represented an even greater change in design methods and the cognitive circumstances of design than that resulting from the introduction of CAD. Whereas previously people had drawn on their monitors in much the same way as on a drawing board, now they tended more to model and then took the designed model apart in the form of descriptive drawings. The new methods of digital modeling allowed a different kind of interplay between digital and analogous models in that, for example, real models could be scanned and then digitally processed, or computer models could be plotted in 3D and thus examined in reality. The interface between digital design and real building still remains largely unresolved, even though now Rapid Prototyping offers a view of a future in which the transition from the metaphor of the drawing board to building in the computer will not be restricted to the architect's office but will be continued on the building site.

The effects of tools

There is one principal reason why, even today in the 21st century, pitched roofs, generally with a slope of 45 degrees, are still built. This reason is not a functional one – we can now build flat roofs –, nor a sentimental one – historical roofs are generally considerably less steep than 45 degrees –, but a geometrical one: 45 degrees is half of a right angle (WOLFF-PLOTTEGG). The two shorter sides of a right-angled triangle are the same length and thus can be easily worked out, and one of the two standard set squares, a widely used drawing tool, has two 45 degree angles. This privileged status of the half right-angle also exists in CAD, where people still often design in orthogonal space.

But does the normative design strength of the tools, what Flusser calls "models of experience" (FLUSSER 1989: 2), really play such an important role in determining the appearance of the built environment? The example of the architect Antoni Gaudí suggests the opposite. In his architecture Gaudí attempted to use a new language of forms that could not be realised with the geometrical methods and means of calculating available at his time. To do this he developed his own tools, which ultimately allowed forms to be made that only today, with the help of digital technology, can again be made without requiring Gaudí's enormous efforts.

PHOTO: PETER KUBELKA

Tools, therefore, have a pertinacity that not only exerts an influence on the architectural products, that is on the material character of buildings, but also on the ideas behind them. Thus what is sketched as well as the choice of the sketching materials, the pencil and the paper, directly influences the idea that grows more concrete in the course of drawing – only very few architects go to their drawing board with a complete concept in their mind (ROBBINS 1994: 32), most develop their concepts through the interaction between an initially vague idea and the concrete lines made on the paper. It remains to be seen what kind of building forms will achieve a privileged status as a result of the most recent developments such as digital modeling and Rapid Prototyping, in a future when the pitched roof is no longer the central image for architecture.

REFERENCES

Flusser, Vilém (1989) Vom Unterworfenen zum Entwerfer von Gewohntem, in: Intelligent Building, Karlsruhe.

Hambly, Maya (1988) Drawing Instruments 1580–1980, London.

Nedoluha, Alois (1960) Kulturgeschichte des technischen Zeichnens, Wien.

Petroski, Henry (1995) Der Bleistift. Die Geschichte eines Gebrauchsgegenstands, Basel.

Robbins, Edward (1994) Why Architects Draw, Cambridge, MA.

Schodek, Daniel L. (2005) Digital Design and Manufacturing. CAD/CAM Applications in Architecture and Design, Hoboken, NJ.

Wilhelm, Gustav (1990) Joseph Hardtmuth. Architekt und Erfinder 1758–1816, Wien.

Wolff-Plottegg, Manfred in conversations with Elke Krasny, May 2007 and August 2008

... rounder than Giotto's O

Gerhard Vana

The oldest drawing instrument that my grandfather, architect Heinrich Vana (1889–1968), is said to have left behind him, is a small hand-held compass (FIG. 1). He probably used it to draw his notes on the course in "theory of architectural form" that he took — as the first step towards training as an architect in the Academy of Fine Arts — at the Vienna Staatsgewerbe-schule in the second decade of the 20th century. In his notes it says: "in Greek architecture curved profiles were all drawn 'free-hand'. In Roman art and therefore also in the 'Renaissance' they were constructed using a compass."

In scholarly terms this is probably intended to suggest that a certain civilisational decline occurred in artistic culture, when the "free-hand outline as a basis" — the heading to my grandfather's drawings — had to be reproduced geometrically, and the architect's emotional unity with the form, as expressed in the gesture of free-hand drawing, was replaced by the intellect.

"... unfortunately using a compass while lying down is most uncomfortable", El Lissitzky wrote in a letter from his sickbed in 1924 (LISSITZKY-KÜPPERS 1980: 39). We can see the compass that he may have been referring to in a photographic work that is clearly related to designs he made for the Pelikan company around that time (FIG. 2). This compass is a model similar to the one left by my grandfather, (who, incidentally, was not quite one year older than Lissitzky), although somewhat larger. This time-bound tool, generally part of the architect's domain, here creates a relationship that can be grasped in words between international art history and work in a specific region and indicates the very different ways in which the activity of an architect can be understood. Whereas my grandfather, who, quite literally, fitted Loos' description of an architect as "a mason who has learned Latin" (HEINRICH KULKA 1979: 17), and used the compass as an everyday tool, the image by the avant-garde artist Lissitzky shows the compass "woven" so to speak in the artist's open hand, as if the gesture of the "artistic" free-hand drawing were here reconciled with the functional "machine drawing" (CF. RIEDLER 1913). On the squared millimetre paper beneath the hand we see a dynamic line that recalls the track of a comet, which — like the outline in academic architecture — could be constructed with the compass, working from an irrational, free-hand gesture.

Lissitzky also used this photo for his self-portrait "The Constructor" (FIG. 3), where however, like in the poster he made for Pelikan around the same time, (SEE FIG. IN KÜHNEL 1999: 10), he replaced the cosmic gesture with a circle. (TSCHICHOLD 1988: 6) This combination of the human hand and the perfect circle recalls the sheet of paper that Giotto is said to have given to a

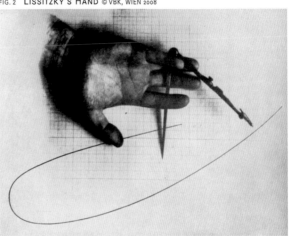

FIG. 2 LISSITZKY'S HAND © VBK, WIEN 2008

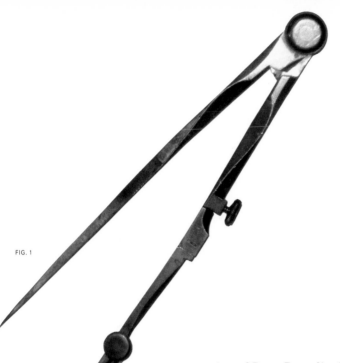

FIG. 1

representative of Pope Benedict XI as a sample of his work: "Giotto, who was very polite, took a sheet of paper and a brush dipped in red paint, positioned his arm firmly at one side, using it like the leg of a compass, and with just a single movement of his hand drew a circle so precise and clear that it must have caused astonishment." (VASARI, NO DATE: 39F)

The calculated provocation of his future patron described in this story about Giotto — Vasari reports that "when this incident became known" it led to the saying "you are rounder than Giotto's O", used by "people of a more coarse kind" (VASARI NO DATE: 40) — is an astonishingly modern gesture, particularly when one holds a geometric reduction of the sheet described in front of one's eyes. El Lissitzky seems to heighten this even further in that he lays aside the artist's attitude and simply takes up the draughtsman's tool. In this context it is remarkable that in a textbook about "machine drawing" such as that by Alois Riedler (or at least in the second edition used in writing this essay) there is a section entitled "Machine Forms, Theory of Form" (RIEDLER 1913: 188FF.) where the concept of the "functional form" is propagated that was later to become popular in architecture under the modified term "functional building" (SEE BEHNE 1926). Riedler here condemns the "childish imitation of nature" (RIEDLER 1913: 194) as found in applied stylistic quotations, which shows that this reflected more the social consensus regarding machine building rather than regarding architecture itself, where elementary geometry was still seen as a provocation. It was only in 1931, in what amounted almost to a reversal of the historical interpretation, that Jakow Tschernikow in his "Konstruktion der Architektur und Maschinenformen" canonised in a graphical monumentalisation the presumed formal principles of machine construction as principles of architecture also (SEE TSCHERNICHOW 1991), curiously divorced from the functional considerations propogated by Riedler.

If we look once again at the ensemble of hand, compass and gesture then modernism's dynamic understanding of form seems here to be connected to the activity of drawing. In "K und Pangeometrie" El Lissitzky quotes an image used, for example, in a very similar way by Kandinsky (KANDINSKY 1973: 57) and Klee (KLEE, 1971: 24), when he relates the line to the movement of a point, ultimately similar to that of a pen or a compass on paper. Lissitzky sensualises the image in a way that goes beyond geometric abstraction when he writes that "a glowing coal in motion leaves behind the impression of a radiant line, and the movement of the material line creates the impression of a surface and a body" (EL LISSITZKY 1925: III). He illus-

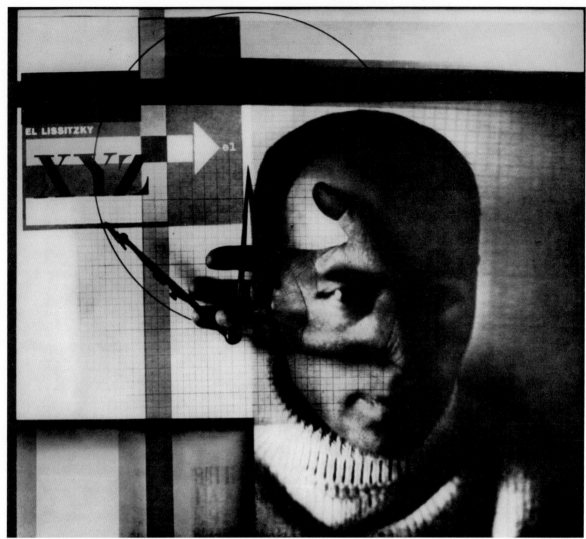

FIG. 3 EL LISSITZKY „THE CONSTRUCTOR" (SELF-PORTRAIT), 1924, © VBK, WIEN, 2008

FIG. 4 IMAGINARY ROTATED FOARM © VBK, WIEN 2008

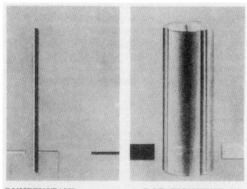

RUHEZUSTAND   ROTATIONSZUSTAND
EL LISSITZKYS IMAGINÄRER ROTATIONSKÖRPER

trates his concept of an "amaterial materiality" (LISSITZKY 1925: 113) by means of imaginary rotated forms. (FIG. 4)

Whereas in the early days of digital plan production in the 1980s one could still hear the curious music of the pen plotter, an acoustic translation of the movements of the drum and the drawing pens (in some cases pencils were even used), today it has been replaced by the montonous background noise of the large format printer. And El Lissitzky's so dynamically created "imaginary space" (LISSITZKY 1925: 111) is now once again "built into a cube" in the monitor and "transformed in such a way that it appears as a pyramid on the surface" (LISSITZKY 1925: 105). Today, when elementary geometry forms part of the basics of every CAD programme it is apparently no longer so artistically productive. Instead once again the complex geometries of organic forms, of the kind often imagined by the Expressionists in their charcoal drawings, have become a model. However, in the way buildings are actually constructed El Lissitzky's paradox of "amaterial materiality" seems at times unresolved.

REFERENCES

Behne, Adolf (1926) Der moderne Zweckbau. München und Wien: Drei Masken Verlag A.G.

Kandinsky, Wassily (1973) Punkt und Linie zu Fläche. Bern-Bümpliz: Benteli.

Klee, Paul (1971) Das bildnerische Denken. Basel und Stuttgart: Schwabe & Co.

Kühnel, Anita (1999) Verführungen. Plakate aus Österreich und Deutschland von 1914 bis 1945 (= Biblos Schriften der ÖNB 174) Umschau/Braus.

Kulka, Heinrich (1979) Adolf Loos. Wien: Löcker.

Lissitzky, El (1925) K. und Pangeometrie (Pp. 103–113) in: Einstein, Carl/ Westheim, Paul (Hg.), Europa Almanach, Potsdam: Gustav Kiepenheuer.

Lissitzky-Küppers, Sophie (1980) El Lissitzky. Maler Architekt Typograf Fotograf. Erinnerungen Briefe Schriften übergeben von Sophie Lissitzky-Küpper. Frankfurt am Main/Wien/Zürich: Büchergilde Gutenberg.

Riedler, Alois (1913) Das Maschinen-Zeichnen. Berlin: Springer.

Tschichold, Jan (1988), Werke und Aufsätze von El Lissitzky (1890–1941), Berlin: Gerhardt.

Tschernichow, Jakow (1991) Konstruktion der Architektur und Maschinenformen. Basel/Berlin/Boston: Birkhäuser.

Vasari, Giorgio (o. J.) Künstler der Renaissance. Wiesbaden und Berlin: Vollmer.

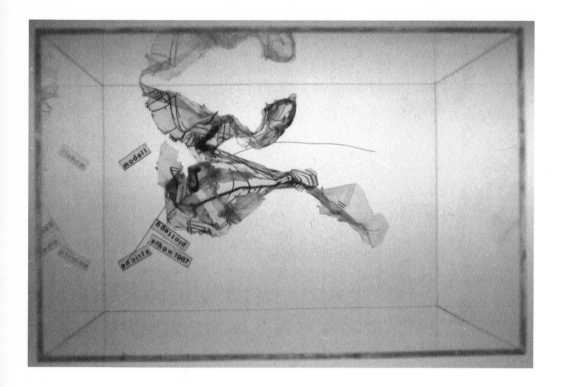

ANALOGOUS ARCHITECTURE GENERATOR,
MANFRED WOLFF-PLOTTEGG
COMPOSITION: Perspex prism 14/21/14 cm,
enclosing 4 spatial patterns (thermo-
mechanically shaped overhead foils), a
polyline (thread), signature, date.
METHOD OF USE: shake vigorously, then put
down quickly (vertically or horizontally); the
resulting "throw" is an architectural design;
several repetitions are recommended.
AREA OF APPLICATION: non-verbal approach
to architecture, to overcome individualistic
form-giving, to transfer creativity to external
processes.
INTERACTIONS: habituation effects occur as
soon as the Limes image is recognised.
SIDE EFFECTS: no matter who throws a new
configuration today, it is already signed by
Plottegg and dated 1987.
If anything is unclear it is recommended that
expert advice be obtained.

Plottegg lines model already 1987
TEXT + PHOTO: MANFRED WOLFF-PLOTTEGG

A LITTLE LEXICON OF TOOLS

The Sketch is regarded as the mythological start of architecture. Sketches often achieve a cult status and become sought-after collectors objects. The sketch is one of the architect's most important design tools and has proved its value as a basis for communication about the design. Hence architects record their first ideas and the following steps for themselves, but also for their staff and clients. What once existed only in the mind is made visible, allowing it to be examined by the designer and others. From the (inner) eye the idea is transferred, by hand, to paper — and back , as what has been defined by drawing then in turn exerts an influence on the original design idea. During discussions with clients sketches are made and are used to explain concepts directly or to respond immediately to clients' suggestions. Whether it be a pencil, ballpoint, felt pen or fountain pen: the instruments used to sketch are light, portable, easy to use and are always at hand when the architect is on the move. Sketches are not made only at the beginning but also during the entire period of working on a project in order to examine changes as well as to try out alternatives and details.

Today software is increasingly used for sketching the first ideas, before the precision of the computer becomes important for making the plans of the building.

PHOTO: ELKE KRASNY

HELSINKI, ALVAR AALTO FOUNDATION

A sketch can be made on any kind of paper. Generally white or yellow sketching paper is used, but notebooks, paper napkins and photocopying paper are also regularly employed. The pencil is the most important and the oldest sketching tool, it has existed since the 16th century in little-altered form. Before this time styli were used to incise, and nibs of lead, silver or copper were employed. The pencil in the form we know it today has existed since the end of the 18th century. At around the same time both the architect Joseph Hardtmuth in Vienna and the inventor Nicolas-Jacques Conté in Paris began experimenting with a mix of graphite and clay and inserted the leads produced in wooden rods. This made pencils more stable and also meant they could be produced in different degrees of hardness. Hardtmuth founded the Koh-i-Noor Hardtmuth pencil factory, which was later to become so famous.

Whereas software was used for a long time only to produce exact plans and to define and draw complex forms, there are now programmes available that can be used to sketch with. These sketches can then be further developed directly by means of CAD (computer-aided design)

Pencil, Tracing Paper & SketchUp

KONRAD GESNER: DE OMNI RERUM
FOSSILIUM GENERE ETC., ZÜRICH 1565
The first depiction of a pencil was published in a book about mineralogy by the Swiss naturalist Konrad Gesner at the time when graphite started to be excavated. Gesner's pencil is a wooden tube in which a pointed piece of graphite was inserted. The knob at one end allowed the pencil to be fixed to a notebook by a string. The image shows the pencil and a piece of graphite, a little-known material at the time. *rt*

SHARPENING A PENCIL,
CATALOGUE A.W.FABER, 1900
The illustration shows sharpening with a penknife using two different methods. In the upper example we see an unpointed pencil, straight from the factory, that is being given a point. *rt*

BOX WITH PENCILS, 1980S
Mechanical pencils have existed since the 19th century. Until the 1970s generally clutch pencils or lead-holders were used which contained graphite leads about 2 to 3 millimetres thick. The mechanical pencil was invented in Japan in 1915 and gave the Sharp Electronics Company its name. The leads are only about 0.2 to 1.4 millimetres thick, the thinnest leads are no longer ceramic but are produced using a polymer admixture. *rt*
VIENNA, COLLECTION ARCH. MOSTBÖCK

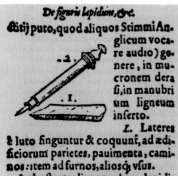

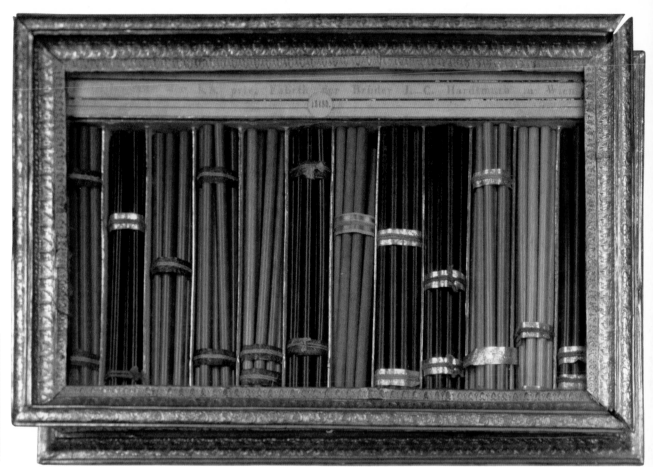

ABOVE CASKET WITH PENCILS, BEFORE 1837
L. & C. HARDTMUTH, VIENNA
Joseph Hardtmuth, architect of the Prince of
Liechtenstein, invented the pencil produced
from ground graphite and clay around 1795.
At the same time the French painter Nicolas
Jacques Conté also worked on a similar
process improving pencils. By that, solidity
was increased — pencils made from graphite
pieces tend to break, especially the poor
quality that was found on the continent.
Additionally, the new method allowed for
producing different varieties of hardness,
depending on the amount of clay added. *rt*
VIENNA, TECHNISCHES MUSEUM, INV. FA-101401

GEDESS LEAD POINTER, 1980S
Mechanical clutch pencils can not be
sharpened with conventional sharpeners.
Special conoid lead pointers for the size of
their leads are used for them. The pencil is
inserted into the lead pointer from above
and is moved circular in such a way that it
describes a cone. Inside the lead pointer,
the lead follows an abrasive surface. The
Gedess lead pointer has been produced
since the late 1930s. *rt*
VIENNA, PRIVATELY OWNED

PENCIL EXTENSION, LATE 20TH CENTURY
A pencil extension is thicker than the pencil
itself and so fits better in the hand. It allows
you to draw even with a tiny pencil stub and
also protects the point when carrying the
pencil around, by concealing it inside the
extension or under a cap. *rt*
VIENNA, VANA-ARCHITEKTEN ARCHIVE

CRETACOLOR 150, 2008
CRETACOLOR HEINRICH SACHS KG, HIRM
The Cretacolor 150 is the successor of the
famous Koh-i-Noor pencil by Hardtmuth. The
latter was varnished in yellow, a reference
to the Austro-Hungarian flag as well as to
the oriental origin of the graphite. Yellow
differed from the competitors' products
then varnished mainly in red or brown. It
was named after the legendary diamond
"Koh-i-Noor" and cost about three times
as much as other pencils. *rt*
HIRM, CRETACOLOR

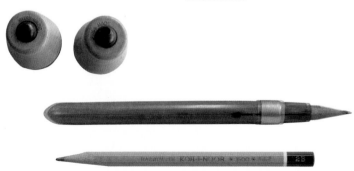

ALVAR AALTO'S 6B CLUTCH PENCIL,
LATE 20TH CENTURY
The clutch pen Versatil ("multi-purpose")
was first introduced by the Czech company
Koh-i-Noor in 1946. The twist-off push
button contains a tiny sharpener.
JYVÄSKYLÄ, ALVAR AALTO ARCHIVE

COPIC MARKERS, LETRASET MARKERS,
AROUND 2000, TOO CORP., TOKYO;
LETRASET LTD., ASHFORD, KENT
Markers are used for sketching and for
presentations. The Copic and Letraset
pens are available in many different colours
and can also be mixed with each other. The
alcohol-based solvent dries very quickly
and attacks neither toner nor ink, which is
one of the reasons for these pens success
from the 1980s onwards. Special pens that
contain just solvent can be used to blend
the colours. rt
VIENNA, PRIVATE OWNERSHIP

SHARPIE, 2008
SANFORD L.P., OAK BROOK, ILLINOIS
The marker known as the Sharpie has
existed since 1964, and is a popular
sketching tool with architects. The Fine
Point has a relatively broad, soft point that
makes lines which remain smudge-free on
very many different materials and have the
characteristic smell of solvent given off by
what are known "permanent markers". rt
VIENNA, PRIVATE OWNERSHIP

COLOURED PENCILS, 1980S, VARIOUS
MANUFACTURERS (JOLLY, BREVILLIER-
URBAN, FABER-CASTELL, STABILO,
HARDTMUTH)
Coloured pencils can be used in a similar
way to normal pencils but the colour means
that they can be used to create watercolour-
like effects. They are produced primarily
from synthetic pigments and wax and they
are dried, unlike lead pencils, which are
fired. Coloured pencils are the modern
equivalent of sepia, red chalk and other
chalks that were made using natural
pigments. rt
VIENNA, ARCHIDELIS

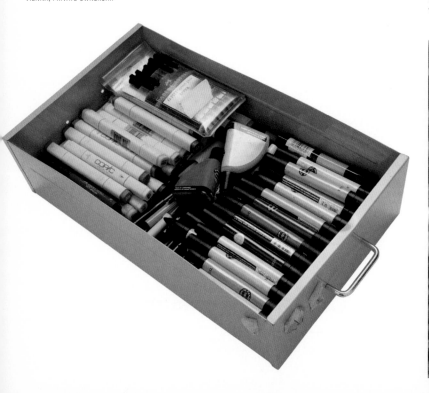

PHOTOS: PETER KUBELKA, ELKE KRASNY

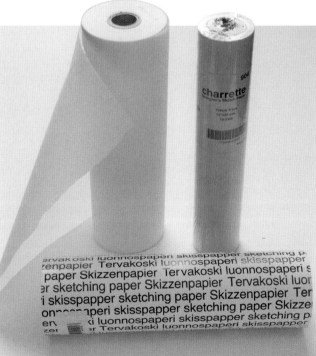

PHOTOS: PETER KUBELKA, ELKE KRASNY

TRACING PAPER, 2008

Light sketching paper is the most important medium used for making sketches with pencil, felt pen or other utensils. The roll is 30 centimetres tall, i.e. roughly the height of an A4 sheet, and about 50 metres long. The paper is transparent and can be easily torn or cut off the roll. Whereas in Europe white sketching paper is dominant, in the USA yellow trace is more widespread. *rt*

VIENNA, PRIVATE OWNERSHIP

GOOGLE SKETCHUP

The name says it all: SketchUp alludes to the traditional act of sketching by hand, even the visual appearance of the programme imitates sketches done by hand. With an easy learning curve compared to other, more sophisticated 3D applications, this programme, originally conceived for architects, is also used in other fields: laypeople like it, because it is easy to understand and Google Earth purchased it and uses it for the building models. *ek*

The plan is a standardised way of depicting architecture and a means of design. The built world was created on the drawing board. From antiquity until the 1950s there were drawing pens, compasses, rulers, and protractors. In 1952 the new mechanical ink pen, the Rapidograph came onto the market. Knives or razor blades were used to "erase" ink lines. Every new decision in a design involved a great deal of drawing and redrawing. In 1980 an appliance was developed for analogous plan lettering, the Scriber. Reproduction, enlarging and reducing in size were all difficult. Now the characteristic smell of ammonia from large print machines has vanished from offices, along with the pantograph used to copy or enlarge images to scale, and the knowledge (once commonplace) about how to spread paper on a drawing board. Copiers have lost their function in reproducing plans and are hardly any longer the playful work tools they once were in the 1980s. From the mid-1980s CAD, computer aided design radically changed the way plans are drawn. The interface between CAD and those who carry out the building remains an unresolved area . The world of building materials is not yet compatible with digital design.

As early as Roman times drawing pens could be produced that, thanks to a flexible ring, allowed lines of different thicknesses to be drawn. Until modern times pens were used to impress or incise lines in the surface of the drawing. These lines were then traced in ink. Drawing pens were used up until the mid-twentieth century in an almost identical form. They were improved around 1700 by an adjusting screw that allowed the line thickness to be adjusted more precisely. And traditional ink was replaced by the more densely coloured and durable Indian ink.

Drawing with a traditional drawing pen required quite some practice — with the introduction of the technical pen things became easier. The Graphos pen by Pelikan became available from the 1930s, after the Second World War the Rapidograph by Rotring was produced along with many similar models. A large range of accessories was available for drawing pens and technical pens: ink, erasing fluid, cleansing fluid and devices. In the 1990s CAD, computer-aided-design, almost completely replaced drawing plans by hand.

Drawing Pens, Razor Blades & CAD

GRAPHOS WITH INSERT NIBS, 1930S,
GÜNTHER WAGNER (PELIKAN), HANOVER
The Graphos, a predecessor of the Rapidograph technical drawing pen, used a large number of interchangeable nibs to draw lines of different widths and kinds. It was filled in much the same way as a fountain pen. From the 1960s onwards a model became available that used ink cartridges. *rt*
VIENNA, VANA-ARCHITEKTEN ARCHIVE

INK CARTRIDGES PELIKAN,
1980S, GÜNTHER WAGNER (PELIKAN),
HANOVER
Ink in different colours to fill mechanical ink pens, drawing pens etc. By exerting pressure on the rubber hemisphere on the bottom the amount of ink can be controlled. *rt*
VIENNA, VANA-ARCHITEKTEN ARCHIVE

OPPOSITE ABOVE
DRAWING INSTRUMENT SAMPLE CASE,
BEFORE 1900, CLEMENS RIEFLER,
NESSELWANG
In 1905 the firm Riefler donated a large display case with all the compasses and drawing instruments they produced to the Deutsches Museum in Munich (which had been founded just a short time previously). Five years previously Riefler had shown this case at the Paris World Exhibition. For the presentation in the museum the instruments were given little cardboard tabs showing the proper technical name and the date each piece was made. *rt*
MUNICH, DEUTSCHES MUSEUM, INV. 3.429

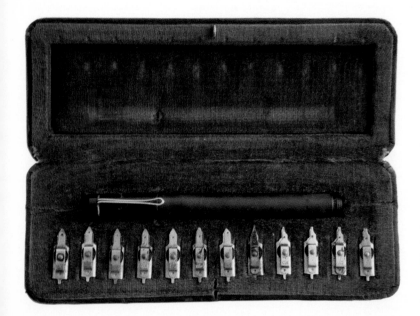

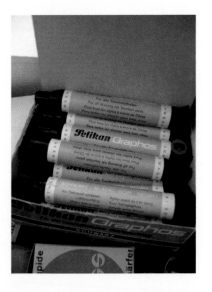

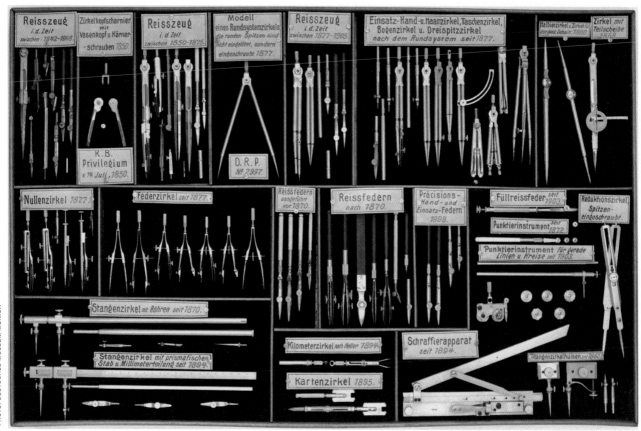

BELOW DRAWING PEN, EARLY 20TH CENTURY
Can be opened for cleaning and has a small wheel to adjust the line width. Drawing an even line with the drawing pen required some practice. In addition the nib had to be re-sharpened regularly, but not too sharp, as that would tear the paper, and in the right form to allow the optimum flow of ink. *rt*

VIENNA, VANA-ARCHITEKTEN ARCHIVE

ALLPLAN BIM, 2008
NEMETSCHEK AG, MUNICH
Nemetschek, a software company that developed from a civil engineering office, has been selling the CAD software Allplan since 1984. BIM, Building Information Modeling, stands for the cross-linking of all information relevant to the building in a digital building model. This makes the courses of the design process and communications with consultants both faster and more efficient. *rt*

AutoCAD
Version 1.0 of AutoCAD was initially released in 1982. In the mid-1980s architects first started to equip their offices with computer workstations, which back then were still very expensive and mostly set up in a separate room, the so called computer room. The last version for Macintosh was released in 1992. CAD libraries offer standardized elements such as doors, walls or windows. AutoCAD, developed and sold by Autodesk, is a vector-based software application for 2D and 3D design. Architectur firms maintain their own CAD libraries consisting of frequently used elements. *ek*

ArchiCAD
Graphisoft, the developer of ArchiCAD, was bought by Nemetschk in 2007. ArchiCAD was launched on Apple Macintosh in 1984, already the first version worked fully in 3D. From the outset the programme was specifically designed to meet architects' needs. The "Virtual Building" creating a database of 3D model data is the heart of the programme. ArchiCAD for students has been made available as free download. *ek*

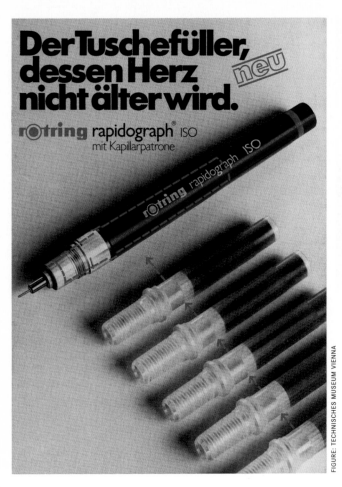

ELECTRICAL ERASING MACHINE, LATE
20TH CENTURY, CHARLES BRUNING
COMPANY INC., CHICAGO, ILLINOIS
Erasing machine to remove ink lines,
machine writing etc. This machine was
filled with special erasing strips. The
button was used to adjust the erasing
speed, according to the kind of strip
being used at the time. *rt*

ROTRING BROCHURE, 1981
ROTRING-WERKE RIEPE KG, HAMBURG
At the beginning of the 1980s Rapidographs
were changed. Conventional ink reservoirs
were replaced by capillary cartridges. These
served for pressure balance as well as to
avoid dripping. *rt*
VIENNA, TECHNISCHES MUSEUM, INV. BPA-010554

DRAWING PEN SET VARIANT/VARIOSCRIPT,
AROUND THE 1960S
ROTRING-WERKE RIEPE KG, HAMBURG
Technical ink pen from Rotring with seven
drawing heads. A further development of
the Rapidograph, first produced in 1959.
The ink was now in a tank that could be
filled and no longer had to be sucked into
the pen by means of a piston. Variant was
intended for drawing and Varioscript for
lettering with stencils. *rt*
VIENNA, ING. GERHARD SCHIER

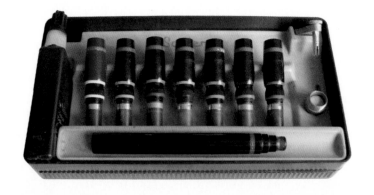

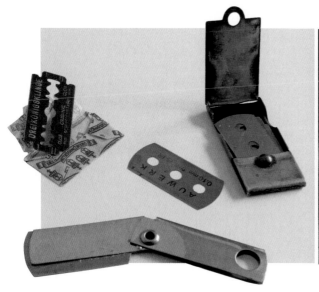

RAZOR BLADES, BOX, HOLDER,
20TH CENTURY
The easiest way of removing ink lines on
tracing paper was to scratch them out using
razor blades — the blades were sometimes
put in special holders or were broken to a
suitable size. To be able to draw again on the
surface where you had scratched something
out you had to smoothen the surface of the
paper, first with an eraser and then with
a blunt instrument such as a bone holder. *rt*

VIENNA, VANA-ARCHITEKTEN ARCHIVE;
VIENNA, ING. GERHARD SCHIER;
HELSINKI, ALVAR AALTO FOUNDATION

DRAFTING BRUSH, AROUND THE 1980S
With ink drawings sometimes a lot of eraser
particles were produced, for instance when,
after inking in the drawing, the preliminary
pencil drawing was erased. The brush was
the gentlest method of removing such
particles. *rt*

VIENNA, COLLECTION ARCH. MOSTBÖCK

ULTRASONIC CLEANER ELTROSONIC,
TYPE 07, AROUND THE 1980S
ELTROSONIC GMBH, WIESBADEN
A major problem with ink pens was that
the tube and the wire in the point became
clogged with paper fibres or dried ink.
To clean them the points were placed in a
water bath in an ultrasonic cleaner whose
vibrations were intended to clear the tube. *rt*

VIENNA, VANA-ARCHITEKTEN ARCHIVE

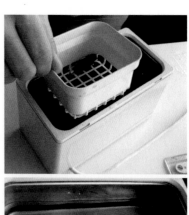

The compass is one of the most ancient drawing instruments and was known to the ancient Egyptians. Compasses were employed both by craftsmen on the building site and by architects. Major improvements in terms of precision were achieved in the 16th century through the use of a curved metal piece or threaded rod that allowed the compass to be finely adjusted. Around this time the first examples were produced in which pencils or styli could be inserted, and the difference developed between compasses used for drawing and dividers with which one could measure, transfer lengths and copy drawings.

Proportional compasses allowed lengths to be subdivided. Beam compasses were used to make large circles. To draw curved shapes such as ellipses, parabolas, hyperbolas or spirals special complex compasses were constructed. Further tools used to draw curves include templates and French curves (such as the Burmester set, which comes from the field of ship-building). Today, thanks to CAD programmes, many curved building forms can be far more easily constructed than in the past.

Compass, Stencil & Indy

COMPASS SET PRÄCISION, 1920S
E.O. RICHTER & CO., CHEMNITZ

Richter patented his "flat system" for compasses in 1892 contrasting with the "round system" patented by his competitor Riefler in 1877 as well as the older three-sided system. After the patent ran out, the flat system was used by most producers since it could be built more efficiently. *rt*

VIENNA, VANA-ARCHITEKTEN ARCHIVE

BEAM COMPASS, EARLY 20TH CENTURY

Two sockets, in which lead points or pens can be inserted, slide along a wooden beam. The form of the beam compass is reminiscent of the oldest method of drawing a circle, i.e. using a point and a string. *rt*

VIENNA, VANA-ARCHITEKTEN ARCHIVE

DRAWING A CIRCLE

How to draw a circle using a compass: you hold the head of the compass and revolve the leg with the pen so that the circle is drawn using just one hand. To ensure that the pen nib touches the paper vertically, the leg must be adjusted to the correct angle at the joint. *rt*

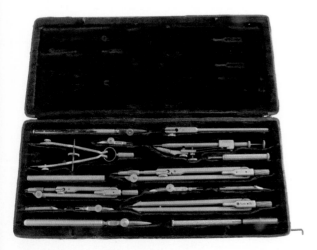

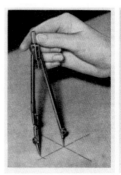

PHOTOS: PETER KUBELKA

PHOTO: ELKE KRASNY

PHOTOS: PETER KUBELKA

BELOW LEFT BURMESTER SET, 1980S
This set of French curves is called after
Ludwig Burmester, who was professor
of descriptive geometry in Dresden and
Munich at the end of the 19th century.
The forms come from the field of
shipbuilding; a set consists of three
templates. It is possible to draw a large
variety of curves with a considerable
degree of accuracy by combining the
different parts. The large template is for
hyperbolas, the smallest one for ellipses,
and the middle one for parabolas. *rt*
VIENNA, VANA-ARCHITEKTEN ARCHIVE

FRENCH CURVES, EARLY 20TH CENTURY
French curves made of plastic and pear
wood – the three wooden curves belong
to range of more than thirty that could
be bought from the drafting equipment
company Gebrüder Wichmann in Berlin
at the beginning of the 20th century. *rt*
VIENNA, VANA-ARCHITEKTEN ARCHIVE;
TECHNISCHES MUSEUM WIEN, INV. 24.194

RIGHT ELLIPSE TEMPLATE, 1990S
STANDARDGRAPH ZEICHENTECHNIK,
GERETSRIED
The corners cut at an angle of 30° allow
this template to be used for the rapid
drawing of ellipses that represent circles
in an isometric projection: the isometric
is a special form of axonometric in which
all the lengths appear foreshortened by
the same amount and the three coordinate
axes are shown at the same angle to each
other. At the bottom right the template
has an isometric of a cube with circles. *rt*
VIENNA, PRIVATE OWNERSHIP

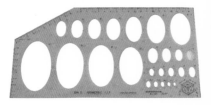

RIGHT ACU-ARC ADJUSTABLE RULER, 1980S,
HOYLE PRODUCTS, INC., GLENNVILLE,
CALIFORNIA
This ruler consists of 14 plastic strips that
are connected to each other by small tracks.
When a particular curve is set it remains
fixed thanks to the friction between the
strips. *rt*
VIENNA, PRIVATE OWNERSHIP

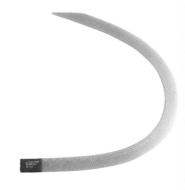

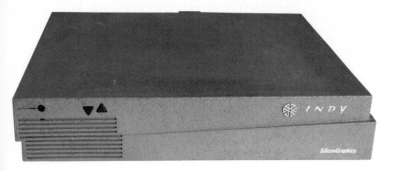

PHOTOS: PETER KUBELKA

INDY, BEGINNING OF THE 1990S
SILICON GRAPHICS, INC. (SGI),
SUNNYVALE, CALIFORNIA
In 1993 SGI brought the computer model
Indy onto the market as an inexpensive,
Unix-based graphical workstation for 2D
und 3D. Initially, thanks to its special
graphics hardware, the Indy was superior
to the PCs available at the time, but after
only a few years it became outdated. CAD
programmes such as AutoCAD ran on the
Indy, as well as animation programmes that
were new at the time. *rt*

VIENNA, PRIVATE OWNERSHIP

PENCIL PLOTTER IP-500EL, 1989
MUTOH INDUSTRIES LTD., TOKYO
Plotter with insert pencils. The pencil is
led along a line across the paper. The sheet
of paper itself is moved at a right angle to
the pencil by the plotter. This means that
every point on the surface of the paper
can be reached. Despite the large drawing
surface of about one square metre the
positioning of the pencil is accurate down
to a fraction of a millimetre. *rt*

VIENNA, VANA-ARCHITEKTEN ARCHIVE

OPPOSITE IVAN SUTHERLAND AND SKETCHPAD
In 1962 at the Massachusetts Institute of
Technology (MIT) Sutherland developed the
predecessor of current CAD programmes,
called the Sketchpad. Here we see him
drawing on the monitor with a light pen.
With the keypad on the left you enter the
commands ("draw", "move"), with the four
dials below the monitor the image can be
shifted. *rt*

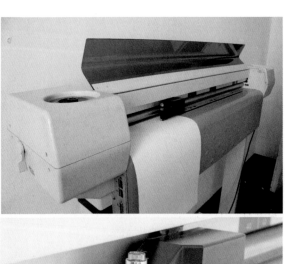

The T-square slides along the drawing board and drawing paper, either with a head that runs along one side of the table or with chords that guide the parallel rule. On this ruler various set squares, angles and rulers are placed to draw lines at the angle required. The building designed is often as orthogonal as the board and ruler. Drawing machines have been constructed since the 17th century. With them a ruler can be positioned at any point on the board and always stays parallel. Later machines were equipped with a rotating head, by means of which lines at any chosen angle could be repeated as often as required. Drawing machines employ counter-weights which fix the ruler and therefore allow drawings to be made at an upright board. Drawing on the computer initially followed the rectilinear grid of the Cartesian system of coordinates. Thanks to increasingly refined graphic processes, today practically all three-dimensional forms can be depicted digitally.

Set-square, T-square & VectorWorks

WOODEN T-SQUARES, 20TH CENTURY
The T-square developed from the carpenter's blade and stock, an adjustable tool used for measuring angles. A T-square is in fact a larger blade and stock in which the stock and the long blade are fixed to each other at an angle of 90°. T-squares of this kind have existed since the 16th century. *rt*
VIENNA, VANA-ARCHITEKTEN ARCHIVE

BELOW WOODEN T-SQUARES IN
ALVAR AALTO'S STUDIO, HELSINKI

PARALLEL STRAIGHT EDGE,
LATE 20TH CENTURY, MAYLINE CO.,
INC., SHEBOYGAN, WISCONSIN
The plastic ruler glides along two cords running along the left and right-hand sides of the drawing board that meet at the upper end of the board. This allows precise adjustment of the ruler on the cords. *rt*
VIENNA, PRIVATE OWNERSHIP

OPPOSITE ABOVE
PARALLELOGRAMM DRAWING MACHINE,
EARLY 20TH CENTURY, ISIS GMBH, GOTHA
The drawing head has two removable scales. They can be adjusted to any desired angle by means of a degree scale. The zero mark can be moved so that drawings can be made using different axis systems. And the screw between the drawing head and the rods allows the direction to be adjusted so that the machine can be fixed on a stretched drawing sheet. *rt*
VIENNA, VANA-ARCHITEKTEN ARCHIVE

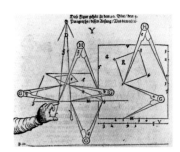

HANS LENCKER: PERSPECTIVA. DARIN EIN LEICHTER WEG ALLERLEY DING IN GRUND ZU LEGEN DURCH EIN SONDERLICHEN INSTRUMENT GEZEIGT WIRD, ULM 1617
At the top left we can see the vanishing point from which cords representing the vanishing lines run across the drawing sheet. The horizontal lengths can be applied directly with the compass at the lower edge of the sheet and projected by means of vanishing lines, the vertical lengths are determined by means of a construction with a diagonal in the square sheet. *rt*

TRIANGULAR SECTION, AROUND THE 1980S ARISTO-ROTRING, WÖRGL
Rulers that show dimensions reduced according to certain scales rather than actual lengths have existed only since the Renaissance. They allowed drawings to be made to specific scales without the need for constant calculations. Triangular rulers have six different scales. Different versions are made for architects, mechanical engineers and cartographers. *rt*
VIENNA, COLLECTION ARCH. MOSTBÖCK

TRIANGLE SET SQUARE, AROUND THE 1990S
The triangle set square comes from the science of navigation and is a combination of ruler, set square and protractor. It can be used to draw straight lines, parallel lines, perpendiculars, lengths and angles. It is a simple, speedy tool that, however, does not always achieve the same precision as large rulers and triangles. *rt*
VIENNA, PRIVATE OWNERSHIP

VECTORWORKS, 2008, NEMETSCHEK NORTH AMERICA, INC., COLUMBIA, MARYLAND
The CAD software VectorWorks was formerly called MiniCAD. MiniCAD was retailed by Diehl Graphsoft from 1985 onwards and was the first CAD software for the Apple Macintosh, which was one year old at that time. After it became available for Windows PCs also from the mid-1990s it was renamed VectorWorks. In 2000 the German producer of Allplan and ArchiCAD bought up Diehl, which is now called Nemetschek North America. *rt*

Since antiquity the simplest method of copying has been by punching drawing points through the paper. For tracing oil was used to make paper transparent. Drawings were also copied by blacking the reverse side and then tracing the resulting lines. The pantograph allowed drawings to be copied, enlarged and reduced in scale. A copying press invented by James Watt with special paint and wet paper was improved to such an extent in the 19th century that it could produce up to 50 copies. Copying pens had to be used.

From 1850 onwards architects used the blueprint: the drawing and the chemically treated print paper beneath it were fixed in a frame and exposed to the sunlight. After they had been developed with water the areas exposed turned blue, the unexposed lines remained white. The copy was thus a negative. From the 1920s onwards the blueprint was replaced by the white print: the printing paper and the drawing on top of it were exposed to UV light and developed using ammonia fumes. The copy was a positive. In 1949 the photo-copier appeared on the market. In addition to allowing limitless enlarging and reducing, the photo-copier's potential as a design tool was also discovered.

Pantograph, Print Machine & Photocopier

ELECTRICAL AUTOMATIC DIAZO PRINTER LPM III, 1920S, CARL JAHODA & BERGMANN, VIENNA
The print paper and the original drawing are led around an upright glass half-cylinder while at the centre the exposure lamp slowly travels down the entire height of the sheet of paper. This appliance, about 2.5 metres tall, exposes automatically, development has to be carried out subsequently. The product was available from the company of Jahoda & Bergmann, based in Vienna since 1911. *rt*
FIG. IN CATALOGUE JAHODA & BERGMANN, VIENNA, 1933

DIAZO PRINTER, 1980S
RIGOLI F.I.M.E. S.P.A., MILAN
The brand name Ozalid that was introduced for the paper used in diazo type printing is the name of the chemical reversed, with one additional letter. After a certain time it began to be widely used as the name for this process, and not just for the products of a company. *rt*
FIG. IN BROCHURE RIGOLI F.I.M.E. S.P.A.

TABLE-TOP COPIER, RICOH FT 2260, 1989
RICOH COMPANY, LTD., TOKYO
The introduction of xerography brought with it new possibilities for reproducing plans. The originals no longer had to be transparent, reductions and enlargements could be easily made and through the effects of contrast and movement the copier became a design tool. Later the copier was also used to transfer lettering produced with the computer to adhesive film. *rt*
VIENNA, VANA-ARCHITEKTEN ARCHIVE

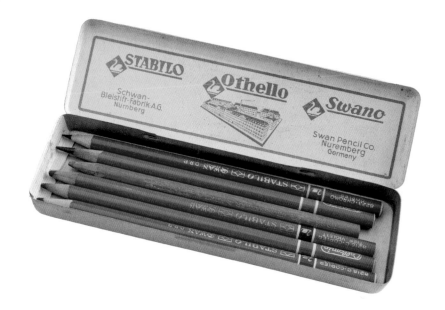

COPY PENCILS, LATE 20TH CENTURY
SCHWAN BLEISTIFTFABRIK AG; H.C. KURZ
KG, BOTH NÜRNBERG
Using copy pencils it was possible, by
means of a copy press, to produce up to
fifty copies of a drawing or a page of text.
The differently coloured copy pencils were
at times used to code different correction
stages. Later they were used only as an
indelible writing tool. *rt*

HIRM, CRETACOLOR

BELOW PANTOGRAPH, CA. 1980
THE LUTZ CO., GUTTENBERG, NEW JERSEY
Simple wooden pantograph. To achieve
certain proportions the two screws must
be positioned in the right holes — ratios
between 1:1⅜ and 1:8 are possible.
Depending upon whether you want to
enlarge or reduce, you draw with either
the middle or outer pen. *rt*

VIENNA, PRIVATE OWNERSHIP

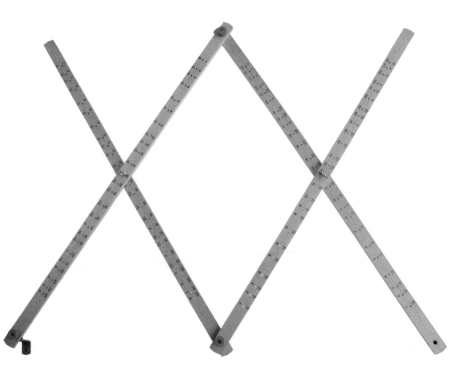

PROPORTIONAL COMPASS, AROUND 1850
KERN & CO AG, AARAU
The adjustable proportional compass can
be used to reduce and enlarge lengths and
figures in proportions set as required. The
dividers allow proportions from 1:10 to
11:12 for lengths. For polygons the radius
of the surrounding circle is entered on one
side of the compass, the other side gives
the length of the sides. *rt*

VIENNA, VANA-ARCHITEKTEN ARCHIVE

Special drawing papers have been available since the end of the 18th century, before this time writing paper was used. From about 1850 onwards industrially produced tracing paper appeared on the market. Plans were often drawn on tracing paper, which allowed corrections to be easily made, and then printed on opaque paper. Before starting to draw the tracing paper was either dampened and fixed using adhesive tape or gum, or pinned with drawing pins. Later crepe tape and transparent adhesive tape were used.

Plans were lettered free-hand using drawing pens, it was only in the 20th century that stencils, transfer letters and lettering machines began to be used. Not just the graphic effect of black lines but also the colouring of plans was always an important theme. In earlier times chalk, watercolours and coloured inks were used that were applied by brush, blow-tube or using mesh through which paint was splattered. Later coloured foils and airbrushes became available, until thanks to CAD it became possible to draw lines and to colour using the same machine, the plotter.

Paper, Letraset & Airbrush

"IDEAL" DRAFTING TABLE, 1930S
CARL JAHODA & BERGMANN, VIENNA
This drafting table can be used sitting down and standing up. It can be adjusted in height and the board itself can be fixed at different angles. A ruler fixed to cords on the left and right of the drawing board can be moved parallel over the drawing, a construction in use since the 17th century. *rt*
TECHNISCHES MUSEUM VIENNA, INV. 72.475

LETTERING STENCILS, 1980S
ROTRING-WERKE RIEPE KG, HAMBURG
Lettering drawings was always a demanding business. With the introduction of tubular nib pens stencils used for lettering were produced to suit different line widths. They were identifiable by a coloured ring that matched the colour coding of the drawing pens. *rt*
VIENNA, VANA-ARCHITEKTEN ARCHIVE

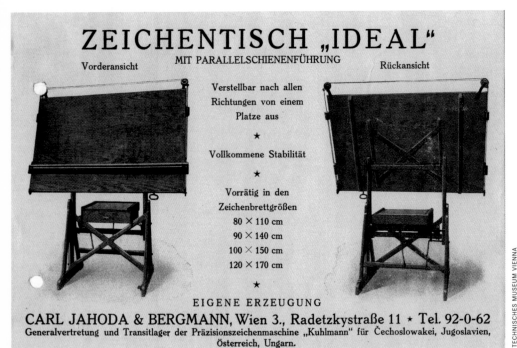

ZEICHENTISCH „IDEAL"
MIT PARALLELSCHIENENFÜHRUNG

Vorderansicht   Rückansicht

Verstellbar nach allen
Richtungen von einem
Platze aus

★

Vollkommene Stabilität

★

Vorrätig in den
Zeichenbrettgrößen
80 × 110 cm
90 × 140 cm
100 × 150 cm
120 × 170 cm

★

EIGENE ERZEUGUNG

CARL JAHODA & BERGMANN, Wien 3., Radetzkystraße 11 ★ Tel. 92-0-62
Generalvertretung und Transitlager der Präzisionszeichenmaschine „Kuhlmann" für Čechoslowakei, Jugoslavien, Österreich, Ungarn.

FIG. TECHNISCHES MUSEUM VIENNA

AIRBRUSH SET AEROGRAPH SPRITE MAJOR,
CA. 1990, ILLINOIS TOOL WORKS, GLENDALE
HEIGHTS, ILLINOIS (DEVILBISS)
The airbrush, a late 19th century invention,
was used from the 1930s onwards, initially
by graphic designers in the USA, and then
made its way to architects' offices. The
completed drawing was covered with
adhesive film, the areas to be coloured
were cut out with a scalpel and then
coloured with the airbrush. *rt*
VIENNA, VANA-ARCHITEKTEN ARCHIVE

DRAWING SET STAMP, 1970S
Identical sets of plans produced by copying
or printing were used, for example, for
building permit applications to local
authorities. Each plan in a particular set
was stamped with an identifying letter so
that one could distinguish between sets
A, B and C. *rt*
VIENNA, VANA-ARCHITEKTEN ARCHIVE

LETTERING MACHINE SCRIBER ET1000,
1980S, MUTOH INDUSTRIES LTD., TOKYO
At the beginning of the 1980s a number of
companies developed what were called NC
scribers (Numerical Control). This appliance
was attached to the drawing machine, an ink
pen was screwed into it, the required text
was entered by pressing the keys, and the
machine then wrote it automatically. There
were also cassettes available with libraries
of symbols containing, for example, items
of furniture. *rt*
VIENNA, COLLECTION ARCH. MOSTBÖCK

DRY TRANSFER AND RUBBING PENS, 1980S,
LETRASET LTD., ASHFORD, KENT, AND
OTHER PRODUCERS
Instead of drawing items of furniture or
fittings by hand using a stencil, Letraset film
could also be used. These were sheets of
plastic film on which the items required
were depicted. They could be inserted in
the drawing by means of dry transfer i.e.
placing them on top of the original drawing
and rubbing over the symbols with a blunt
instrument. *rt*
VIENNA, VANA-ARCHITEKTEN ARCHIVE

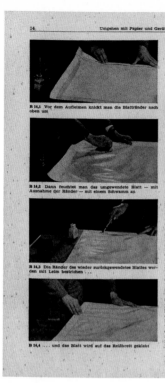

FIXING A DRAWING SHEET, WILHELM
SCHNEIDER: TECHNISCHES ZEICHNEN
FÜR DIE PRAXIS, BRAUNSCHWEIG 1958
The images explain how to fix a sheet of
drawing paper to a drawing board. The sheet
is first dampened so that when it dries it is
stretched taut. *rt*

TECHNISCHES MUSEUM VIENNA, INV. EB 563

BELOW AND OPPOSITE

MARGINALIEN, PETER AUER 1993
What we have here is a sheet, made of
Hallein paper, that was stretched across a
drawing board, on which drawings were
made using a parallel ruler (120 cm long)
made of transparent plastic that ran on
cords on either side of the board. Other tools
used were ink pens (Rotring), pencils, and
adhesive tapes. TEXT: PETER AUER

MARGINALIEN, DETAIL

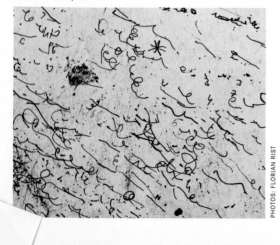

The model plays a variety of roles, both in design or presentation. It helps in understanding spatial effects. Both the materials that can be used, which range from cardboard to Lego, Styropor, Perspex, wood or clay, and the techniques that are employed seem limitless. Simple, rapidly made working models are common, but there are also precise models made to work out spatial details and to depict urban contexts. The working model forms a bridge between the playful approach to form and space, and professional implementation. Often expensive display models are made only in response to a client's wishes.

Thanks to computerisation today we can combine the two and three-dimensional. The interplay between computer, film, cutter or 3D plotter produces complex new possibilities of visualisation. Models are built and animated on the computer – animations are used both to crystallise form and to produce "walk-throughs". 3D inkjet printers are operated by computer and build up real models out of layers of powder. A variety of CNC machines (Computer Numerical Control) such as cutters, mills, drills, saws and presses are used to make models, but also in the production of building elements directly from the computer.

Even the simplest of means such as sheets of cardboard or blocks of Styropor are adequate design tools. It seems that for a long time models were used primarily to present projects or explain designs to building craftsmen — as the wonderful wooden examples by Brunelleschi and Michelangelo indicate — rather than as design tools. In the 20th century models were cut out of materials such as wood or Styropor, modelled out of clay or Plasticine, cast in metal or plaster, or pieced together out of paper, cardboard, plastic, wood or metal sheets.

Nowadays models are increasingly produced as 3D objects in the computer and shown on the monitor. Using various technologies models are automatically produced from these digital originals through milling, 3D plotting or by cutting panels that are then pieced together. Real models are scanned to allow further work to be carried out on the digital model, which can then later become a real model once again.

Stanley Knife, Glue & 3D Plotter

FOAM CORE BOARD AND PINS,
MDV PAPIER- UND KUNSTSTOFFVER-
EDELUNG, KARLSTEIN, GERMANY
Depafit foam core boards combine the advantages of hard foam and cardboard. They are available in thicknesses of 3, 5 and 10 millimetres, that is to say relatively thin, but stiffer and more three-dimensional than cardboard. They can be cut precisely with a knife, mitred corners can also be made with them, and they can be either glued together or joined with pins. *rt*
VIENNA, ARCHIDELIS

CUTTING MAT AND SCALPEL,
STANDARDGRAPH ZEICHENTECHNIK,
GERETSRIED; MARTOR KG, SOLINGEN
To protect tabletops and to keep knives and blades sharp special cutting mats are used that consist of a minimum of three layers of plastic: on each of the outer faces a layer of soft PVC, in the middle harder PVC. Scalpels are used for particularly fine cutting work in model building but also in plan drawing and layouting. *rt*

OPPOSITE ABOVE NEEDLES, DRAW PLATES,
CHISELS, TWEEZERS
Model building is always largely a matter of improvisation. For various cutting, scoring, pricking and other operations model builders produce special metal tools that are then set in a wooden handle, and use chisels. Tweezers are used to pick up and hold small parts. *rt*
VIENNA, ARCHIDELIS

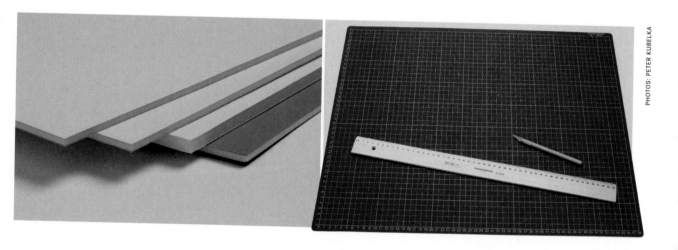

PHOTOS: PETER KUBELKA

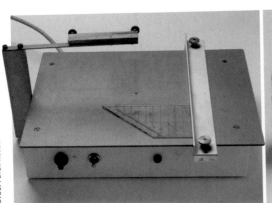

HOT WIRE CUTTER BM4, AROUND 1980
BURKHARDT, MUNICH
Hard foam polystyrene panels can be easily
cut with a heated wire. This small thermal
cutting appliance from the early days has
a working surface and a guide. The cutting
is done by means of wire that is set under
a 12 volt current and is heated to glowing
point by electrical resistance. To cut the
piece of hard foam it is fed against the
glowing wire, much in the same way as
a band saw is used. *rt*

VIENNA, ARCHIDELIS

METHYLEN CHLORIDE
Methylen chloride or dichlormethane
is a chlorocarbon that smells much like
chloroform. In model building it is used to
join pieces of acrylic — as it creates invisible
joints — and polystyrene sheets. This chemical
is applied with a brush and attacks the plastic
so that, when two parts of the building model
are pressed together, the plastic melts rapidly,
creating what is called a plastic weld. *rt*

VIENNA, ARCHIDELIS

PROTECTIVE MASK, 1990S
SHIROHATO CO., LTD., NAGOYA
Avoiding contact with dangerous solvents
and dust when building models is almost
impossible. Special masks with dust filters
are used as protection against dust — this
Japanese mask is one such example. *rt*

VIENNA, PRIVATE OWNERSHIP

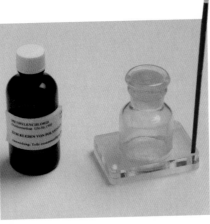

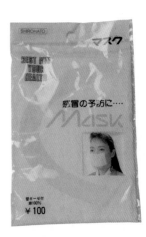

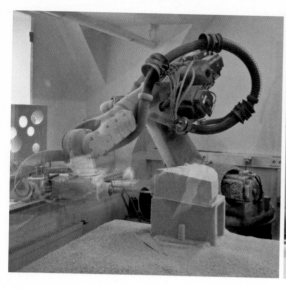

PHOTOS: FLORIAN RIST

UTILITY OR STANLEY KNIVES, 1990S
One of the most important model building tools is the Stanley knife, named not after the British producer of drafting instruments but after the American tool producer Stanley Works. The original Stanley knives are used for handcraft and have exchangeable blades, whereas architects use models with long segmented blades. When the edge becomes dull it can be snapped off, exposing a new sharp edge. *rt*

VIENNA, PRIVATE OWNERSHIP

INDUSTRIAL ROBOT KR 60 HA, 2000S, KUKA AG, AUGSBURG
The use of multiple axis industrial robots increases the possibilities of digital model building. This robot has six axes; a seventh is achieved by means of a rotating object plate. Standard CNC mills generally have three operable axes. A greater degree of freedom allows more complicated and also undercut forms to be produced. In addition to a milling tool the robot can use a variety of other tools. *rt*

VIENNA, UNIVERSITY OF TECHNOLOGY, INSTITUTE OF ART AND DESIGN

PHOTO: PETER KUBELKA

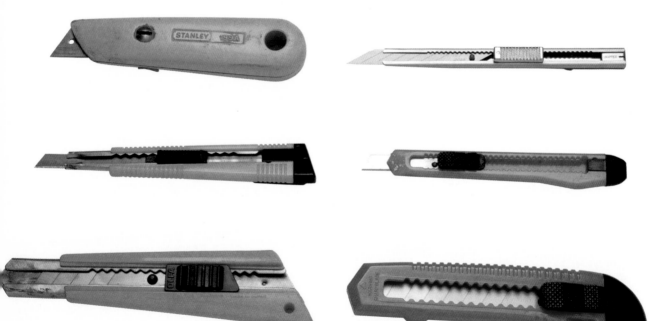

PLASTICINE
Models are not only made up of elements or cut out of blocks of materials but are also made using malleable materials such as plaster, clay or Plasticine. For professional use there is clay (industrial Plasticine), which, in contrast to the children's play materials, is harder and generally brown in colour and can be worked with tools when cold. But standard Plasticine can also be used for models, especially where colour is important. *rt*

VIENNA, PRIVATE OWNERSHIP

MICROSCRIBE G2X, 2000S
IMMERSION CORP., SAN JOSE, CALIFORNIA
This system allows the digitising of real objects. Points or contours traced with the tip are recorded three-dimensionally then, by means of software, surfaces and volumes can be calculated from them so as to create a digital 3D copy of the analogous model. *rt*

VIENNA, UNIVERSITY OF TECHNOLOGY,
INSTITUTE OF ART AND DESIGN

The profoundest change for the creation of architecture is the move from 2D to 3D which affects not only design but also drawing and documentation, the increasing creativity gap and the spiraling curve of expected speed and hyperefficiency. The potential of a changing design vocabulary in the production lies in computer aided production as well as innovative materials which unfold their specific, and often still surprising, material qualities through the process of production.

The culture expressed through programmes and software varies widely: open source and individual scripts next to costly software with demanding learning curves, easily reproduced standardized elements next to the difficulty of individualized creation within the wide gamut of forms that can be generated.

On principle, the begin of the 21st century is marked by a trend towards an expanded range of tools characterized by the coexistence of tradition and innovation: pencils and tracing paper is combined with 3D modeling, scanners, 3D plotters and render engines.

3D Modeling, Bézier Curves & Render Engines

ADOBE PHOTOSHOP

The Knoll brothers, Thomas and John, began working on an image editing programme called Display in 1987. As early as 1910 photomontages were used in architectural competitions: a photo of the architectural model was placed in the rendering of the building site to give a realistic impression of the future building. In the 1950s architects still belittled the use of photomontages by Yona Friedman as a means of expression for laymen. In 1988 the Knoll brothers sold the licence to Adobe and wrote software history. Today's architectural practice is unimaginable without Adobe Photoshop by Adobe Systems. *ek*

ADOBE ILLUSTRATOR

This vectorbased drawing programme was developed for Macintosh by Adobe Systems and first released in 1987. The very first versions had basic features only. Adobe Illustrator offers a good example of how recent technological moves reflect and mimic older tools: since 1993 there are paint buckets, knives or calligraphic paintbrushes to be found on the toolbar. In 1997 a windows version was introduced. *ek*

CATIA

Catia stands for Computer Aided Three-Dimensional Interactive Application and is a 3D modeling program originally developed for airplane design by the French company Dassault Systèmes, marketed by IBM. In 1969 Avions Marcel Dassault set out to develop a graphic programme for drawing. The latest version Catia V5 is a parametric 3D CAD programme used in automobile and airplane design and manufacturing, electronics, construction, medicine as well as furniture design but also in toolmaking, modelmaking or architecture. Catia is part of the Alpha Jet as well as the Guggenheim Museum in Bilbao. *ek*

CINEMA 4D, 2008

Cinema 4D is a programme for 3D modeling and animation developed by the German company Maxon, part of the Nemetschek Group since 2000. The first version of the predecessor FastRay was launched in 1991 for Commodore Amiga. Cinema 4D is used for large animation cinema films, but also in architecture and design. *rt*

SCANNER

In the 1980s the xerox machine was an ordinary tool in architects' offices, which through deliberate misuse, by shaking, pounding, pushing or scaling up or down set free its inspirational qualities for the design process. Today, in very different ways though, the technological process of scanning provides unexpected and surprising insights into space or even evokes design inspirations. Nowadays any type of object can be placed on the a glass window of flatbed scanners and turned into a digital image. *ek*

3DS MAX

3Ds Max is an application for 3D modeling, animation, rendering and visual effects currently in its 11th version and developed further by Autodesk. Films and video games are made with help of 3Ds Max but it is also widely used in architecture and design. It was originally developed by Kinetix under the name of 3D Studio Max. In order to obtain a high degree of realism renderings use multiple reflections or lighting based on geo coordinates changing according to the time of year or the time of day. *ek*

FORM.Z

The software company auto.des.sys introduced form.Z in 1991. Today's design vocabulary marked by nonorthogonality, warped forms or blobs is regarded as prototypical expression of computer aided design. However, warping or curved surfaces, were an actual challenge and most time consuming in the early days of CAD. Today this 3D graphic software is used for 3D modeling, animation, rendering and construction. From Bézier curves, named after Pierre Étienne Bézier, who first used them to design automobile bodies at Renault and used today to model smooth curves that can be scaled indefinitely, to parametric objects, form.Z allows for 2D as well as 3D form manipulation. *ek*

MAYA

Most Advanced Yet Acceptable is what the acronym Maya, a software first introduced in 1998, stands for. On one hand automotive design as well as airplane design are the engines of innovation when it comes to a technology transfer into the field of architecture. On the other hand it is the film and video game industry which is pushing the digital technology then also entering the architectural field. Maya is a highly complex, integrated node-based 3D computer graphics and 3D modeling software characterized by modular openness for plug-ins used for visualisations and animation. In 2006 the software originally developed by Alias Systems Corporation was purchased by Autodesk. *ek*

RENDERN

The almost true to life appearance of not yet built architecture is almost exclusively linked to the computer term render. But renderings are a lot older than computers. Sketches or plans done by hand with pencil or ink were worked on with colour pencil or chalks to highlight shadow effects as natural as possible. The result was called a rendering. Today materials are scanned and then used for renderings to make them appear more realistic. When it comes to architectural visualisations clients' expectations are ever increasing. This has led to new demand answered by companies specialized in visualisation which in turn led to a new problematic concerning the issues of authorship and intellectual property rights in architects since these specialists claim copyright to the images produced showing architecture created by somebody else entirely. *ek*

REVIT ARCHITECTURE

The building design software Revit Architecture offers better and faster coordination between the disciplines, between designers and contractors. Designing, building and documenting moves into 3D and becomes fully interrelated. Information is automatically updated via BIM, Building Information Modeling. Computational design not only has an impact on the design vocabulary, but, considering the long-term effects, maybe even more importantly on the given time frames of making architecture. *ek*

RHINOCEROS

Rhinoceros, often colloquially shortened to Rhino, is a freeform modeling instrument for industrial design, architecture, jewellery design als well as rapid prototyping translating digital data directly into workpieces without any other in-between steps. The software was developed by Robert McNeel & Associates and originally an open source which was collectively improved by many users. Rhino's scripting language uses Visual Basic Script. Rhino's popularity is not only due to its relative cost-effectiveness, but also because Rhino is a powerful converting instrument between various programmes in a design process. *ek*

MAXWELL RENDER

The special feature of the stand-alone-renderengine Maxwell Render is the physically correct simulation of light. The perfection of the photorealistic, true-to-life simulation works with physically correct light sources using the spectral waves of the light and not the computerbased RGB colour spectrum. The interrelatedness and confluence of computer programmes lies in their plug-in structures: Plug-ins for Maxwell Render for example exist for 3dsMax, Allplan, ArchiCAD, AutoCAD, Cinema 4D, formZ, Houdini, Lightwave, Maya, Rhino, SketchUp, und Solidworks. *ek*

GEHRY TECHNOLOGIES

In 2002 Frank Gehry founded Gehry Technologies GT. This is a recent example of an architect yet again to change the tools for the architecture profession. Following the example of product design and production which had already earlier been profoundly transformed and made the move into 3D, Gehry Technologies is accelerating the trend into 3D. Research and development are carried out with academic institutions as well as the industry: MIT's Media Laboratory, Georgia Tech and CERF. Product development is carried out jointly with IBM as well as Dassault Systems, the developer of Catia. Gehry Partners have largely pioneered model-centric design which is in turn driving technology initiatives and software development changing the practice of architecture. GT's Digital Project offers 3D Building Information Modeling (BIM) and management tools and uses Catia as a core engine. *ek*

web: archidelis.at

BIG Bundes
Immobilien
Gesellschaft

Architektur beginnt im Kopf ...

gemeinsam schaffen wir daraus

Raum für die Zukunft!

Als Österreichs wichtigster Immobilien-
besitzer und Bauherr legt die BIG neben
kommerziellen Interessen verstärkt auch
auf baukünstlerische Qualität großen
Wert.

Wirtschaftlichkeit und Architektur
gehen Hand in Hand.

Bundesimmobiliengesellschaft m.b.H
Hintere Zollamtsstraße 1, 1031 Wien
T +43 5 0244-0, F +43 5 0244-2211

office@big.at, www.big.at

Contributors' Biographies

Dietmar Steiner

Dietmar Steiner, born in 1951. Studied architecture at the Academy of Fine Arts in Vienna.
Until 1989 he held a teaching post in architecture history and theory at the Hochschule für angewandte Kunst in Vienna. Dietmar Steiner has been director of the Architekturzentrum Wien since 1993.
In 2002 he curated the Austrian contribution to the Architecture Biennial in Venice in his capacity as Commissioner.
He is a member of the advisory committee for the European Union Prize for Contemporary Architecture — Mies van der Rohe Award, the most significant European architecture award, as well as being president of ICAM — International Confederation of Architectural Museums — the umbrella organisation for architecture museums world-wide. In addition, Dietmar Steiner works as an architecture consultant on a number of juries and for a number of appraisals. His many years' editorial experience with the Italian journal 'domus' and many published articles on the topics of architecture and urban development are also among his activities.

Elke Krasny

Cultural theorist, curator, author, art and culture projects in public and social space; works, researches, curates, teaches and publishes along the connections between architecture, art as public space, urbanism, gender and representation, as well as museums and exhibitions in cultural formations; lecturer at Vienna Academy of Fine Arts, Ernst-Georg-Heinemann Foundation visiting professor at Bremen University on the theme of "Paths into the City. The Narratives of Urban Transformation" 2006, lecturer at Salzburg University 2008 on the theme: "City Space Gender — the Production of Urban Narratives. Critical Reflection as Intervention"; Her book for children and young people, Warum ist das Licht so schnell hell?, was awarded the Austrian Prize for Books for Children and Young People.
PUBLICATIONS AUTUMN 2008: Stadt der Frauen. Eine andere Topographie von Wien, Wien Metro Verlag 2008; Urbanografien. Stadtforschung in Architektur, Kunst und Theorie, eds. Elke Krasny, Irene Nierhaus, Berlin Reimer Verlag 2008; Unsere Welt in den Augen der Welt. Identität und Authentizität als Frage der Gestaltung im Medium Weltausstellung, in: Matthias Götz (Hg.) Villa Paragone. Thesen zum Ausstellen, Basel Schwabe Verlag 2008.

Gudrun Hausegger

Studied medicine, history of art and architecture in Graz, Vienna and Los Angeles (2000–2003 masters degree course at the University of California, Los Angeles). 1996–1998 press and archive work with Coop Himmelb(l)au, 1998–2000 lectureship at the University of Applied Arts in Vienna. 1998–2000, and once again since 2004, project management in the ArchitekturzentrumWien. Her research work focuses in particular on European and US-American architecture from 1940 to the present. Publications in the framework of Coop Himmelb(l)au and the Architekturzentrum Wien.
PUBLICATION: Steven Holl. LOISIUM: World of Wine, Hatje Cantz 2007.

Robert Temel

is a self-employed researcher, journalist and communicator in the areas of architecture, the city and cultural theory. He examines the field of planning from a perspective than includes design and functional aspects as well their broader contexts – which is to say he also takes into account the roles played by politics and administration, clients and users, business and society. Since 2003 Temel has been chairperson of the steering committee of the Österreichische Gesellschaft für Architektur (ÖFGA). PUBLICATIONS: Florian Haydn, Robert Temel (eds.): Temporary Urban Spaces. Concepts for the Use of City Space, Basel 2006; Robert Temel: Temporärer Urbanismus. Potenziale begrenzter Zeitlichkeit für die Transformation der Städte in: Elke Krasny, Irene Nierhaus (eds.) Urbanografien. Stadtforschung in Kunst, Architektur und Theorie, Reimer Verlag Berlin 2008.

Gerhard Vana

1988–1992 university lecturer at the Institute of Art and Design of the TU Vienna (Vienna University of Technology), department of sculptural design and model building, 1992–1996 assistant professor and director of the research project "Baukästen" (Building Kits), 1994 obtained his doctorate in technical sciences at the TU Vienna (with distinction), 1994–2001 lecturer on "The Architectural Model" at the TU Vienna, 1996 awarded his licence as "Staatlich befugter und beeideter Ziviltechniker" (state certified engineer), since then has worked as a self-employed architect with his office in Vienna, 2001–2003 took part in the conception and execution of the research project: "Architektur und Baukasten" (Architecture and Building Kits) as a free-lance expert assistant. 1984 Swiss steel building promotion award 2nd prize, 1986 Karl Scheffel memorial prize of the Zentralvereinigung der Architekten Österreichs.

ALVAR ALTOS YARDSTICK
JYVÄSKYLÄ, ALVAR AALTO ARCHIV

Acknowledgements

Anita Aigner
Marc Albertin
Garrick Abrose
Wendy Arrington
Philipp Aschenberger
Heinrich Auer
Peter G. Auer
Joan Bassegoda Nonell
Corinne Bélier
Ben van Berkel
Marlies Breuss
Steward Berriman
Ewald Bilonoha
Gerhard Binder
Chantal Bittrich
Emile Boucheteil
Dirk Bühler
Carla Camilleri
Alfred Candrian
Mary Chan
Gary Chang
Haiko Cornelissen
Mónica Cruz Guáqueta
Dana Cuff
Hermann Czech
Kersu Dalal
Alexander Desbulleux
Rodolfo Dias
Johanna Diehl
Ingrid Diem
Elizabeth Diller
Nermin Dizdarevic
Robert Donnelly
Clemens Ellmauthaler
Annemarie Emeder
Anneke Essl
Michael Etzel
Solange Fabiãio
Jordi Faulí i Oller
Barbara Feller
Marianne Fischbacher
Ingrid Fitzek
Colin Franzen
Yona Friedman
Françoise Fromonot
Martina Frühwirth
Martina Fuchs
Birgit Gartner
Nick Gelpi
Ben Gilmartin

Judy Glass
Wolfgang Gleissner
Eugenia Gorini Esmeraldo
Rainer Graefe
Susanne Gronemann
Wolfgang Hammerer
Marja-Liisa Hänninen
Harald Hasler
Gregor Harbusch
Gudrun Hausegger
Wolfgang Heidrich
Arne Heporauta
Marta Hernàndez i Roig
Steven Holl
Marjo Holma
Yvonne Hotwagner
Helmut Houdek
Dorothee Huber
Herbert Hutterer
Yoshiko Iwasaki
John Izenour
Kristof Jarder
Ben Jakober
Familie Jochum
Momoyo Kaijima
Gabriele Kaiser
Susanne Kappeler-Niederwieser
Barbara Katzelmayer
Armin Keck
Hollyamber Kennedy
James Kolker
Machteld Kors
Erhard Krasny
Yamna Krasny
Bernadette Krejs
Peter Kubelka
Thomas Kussin
Marion Kuzmany
Gyoung Nam Kwon
Esa Laaksonen
Anne Lacaton
Helmut Lackner
Rosmarie Ladner
Alicia LaDuke
Stephanie Lavaux
Vivian Lazzareschi
Sonja Lebos
Alfred Lechner
Catherine Lecoq
David van der Leer

Thomas Liedl
Karin Lux
Peter Märkli
Alexandra Maringer
Fernando Marzá Pérez
Aude Mathé
Daniel McCoubrey
Chris McVoy
Gabriele Metzger
Andreas Mieling
Herbert Mödlhammer
Anita Mostböck
Martin Mostböck
Karen Murphy
Vezio Nava
Ute Neuber
Irene Nierhaus
Andrea Nussbaum
James Roderick O'Donovan
Michael Ogertschnig
Andrew Ogilvie
Alessandro Orsini
Katariina Pakoma
Pernette Perriand Barsac
Hartmut Petzold
Alexander Pirker
Sonja Pisarik
Monika Platzer
Manfred Wolff-Plottegg
Markus Puchberger
Ines Purtauf
Charles Renfro
Ursula Riederer
Johann Riegler
Florian Rist
Katharina Ritter
François Roche
Nancy Rogo Trainer
Christian Roschitz
Mario Rosner
Angelica M. Ruano
Ulrike Ruh
Peter Sauerwein
Susan Scanlon
Georg Schwalm-Theiss
Ricardo Scofidio
Denise Scott Brown
Hans-Peter Siffert
Martin Skladal
Werner Skvara

Monika Sparta
Evelyn Spindler
Klaus Stattmann
Dietmar Steiner
Oscar Steiner
Hester Stöbe
Marcelo Suzuki
Heinz Schalk
Gerhard Schier
Christoph Schlosser
Beate Schnitter
Lutz Schöbe
Cornelia Schörg
Alexander Schuh
Yaron Schuh
Yona Schuh
Leon van Schaik
Michael Schöller
Martin Schwanzer
Christoph Stadlhuber
Lek Thanavatik
Robert Temel
Jeremy Tenenbaum
Andreas Thierer
Eamon Tobin
Jos Tomlow
Monika Tscholakov
Yoshiharu Tsukamoto
Nia Turner
Gerhard Vana
Jean-Philippe Vassal
Robert Venturi
Alexandra Viehhauser
Sílvia Vilarroya
Malu Villas Bôas
Laia Vinaixa
Alexandra Wachter
Ute Waditschatka
Daniel A. Walser
Torsten Warner
Daniel Weiss
Mark Wigley
Ebbie Wisecarver
Noah Yaffe
Ute Woltron
Sandy Yu
Michael Zinganel